# CHESTER TO

# CHEPSTOW

## Journal of a Bike Journey

## JOHN DAVIES

First Published in 2007 by:
Pneuma Springs Publishing

John Davies has asserted his/her right under the Copyright, Designs and Patents Act, 1988, to be identified as Author of this Work

Pneuma Springs Publishing
A Subsidiary of Pneuma Springs Ltd.
7 Groveherst Road, Dartford Kent, DA1 5JD.
E: admin@pneumasprings.co.uk
W: www.pneumasprings.co.uk

A catalogue record for this book is available from the British Library.

## APPRECIATIONS

*Thanks to:*

*Ad, my understanding wife.*

*Ian, my son who set me on the path.*

*And in time-honoured alphabetical order:-*

*Geraint Davies, Hefin Elis, Geraint Griffiths, Dafydd James, Euros Lewis, Sian Orrells, Frank Watkins and all the people I spoke to on my journey.*

# January 2006

*There was an old man from Glamorgan*

*Who could not play a tune on the organ*

*So he got on his bike*

*And round Wales did hike*

*Till he returned once again to Glamorgan*

$Q$uite unexpectedly on a dreary January day my son, Ian, said to me, "Hey Dad, what about that bike ride you've been talking about? When are you going to do that?" Good question, when am I going to do it?

It's something I'd thought about for many years, but other things kept getting in the way. It lodged in my mind though, so after a few days gestation I decided to start planning for it straight away. After all, at 57 years of age with the old knees playing up, if I left it any longer I'd probably never do it.

The journey was initially a vague notion of getting to somewhere in North Wales by public transport, then somehow cycling back home to Port Talbot. After a bit more thought I decided to cycle from Chester to Chepstow. Not the direct north-south route, but roughly following the Welsh coastline along the north coast through Anglesey, Llyn, Cardigan Bay, Pembrokeshire and eastward across the south coast.

I worked for BP Chemicals in Baglan Bay for more than 30 years. For the last 16 of those years I cycled to work come rain or shine. The bikes I owned at this time were a Raleigh mountain bike and a GT lightweight road racer. Neither of them were suitable for the trip I'd planned, so this meant buying a new one specifically designed for touring.

I'm not an expert on bicycles, I just enjoy riding them. I had no experience of touring at all, that was why I contacted my old friend Geraint Griffiths. He is a Veteran of many cycling trips to Ireland, amongst other places, and was able to offer me some good advice.

I first met Geraint back in 1960 when we both attended Glanafan Grammar School in Port Talbot. Our mutual interest in music and cycling brought us together. We rode many miles together and in 1965 joined a short-lived rock band where Geraint first displayed his considerable talent as a singer and guitar player. We couldn't decide on a name for the band so we became 'The Undecided'. My budding career as a rock star ended with the demise of the band. Geraint went on to become a much-respected star of Welsh language music, television and radio.

# *February*

*I* drove to Carmarthen where Geraint enlightened me on the difference between touring and everyday cycling. He gave me a guided tour of his custom made bike which cost more than £1,000 back in 1995 and also a  comprehensive list of what I'd need for my trip.

Happy with my new-found knowledge, the following morning I dusted down my old mountain bike, wrapped up well against a temperature of only 2°C and began training for my bike journey around Wales. That first day I cycled only eight miles because of the cold weather, but it was a start.

I'm fairly fit for my age because I run every day, unless I'm ill or injured. It was merely a question of getting bike fit again. I've been a member of Port Talbot Harriers since 1983 and still enjoy competing in a variety of events from cross country to throwing the javelin. I particularly enjoy the veteran competitions because of the strong sense of comradeship as we get older and slower together. My motivation to keep fit is what got me started, the fact that it's become a habit is what keeps me going.

It was obvious that I needed a proper touring bike. An internet search on Google threw up a bewildering array of sites for bikes, so I settled for the names I knew like Raleigh and Dawes. The local shops didn't have much stock in as they claimed it was too early in the season. Surfing the net, though, did give me a feel for the prices and what was available.

At this stage I realized that I was intending to leave home on my own for perhaps a couple of weeks. Adrianne, my long-suffering wife of 34 years, had quietly accepted the fact that a man's gotta do what a man's gotta do. In fairness I did offer to buy a tandem so she could come too. That offer was declined, so the search was on again for a standard one man bike. It's easy to find grounds for divorce. The trick is to find grounds for staying together. In fact, I don't know how Ad has put up with me for so long.

The internet revealed some basic touring bikes for about £300. Then there were some high spec models costing thousands. I was aiming for reasonable quality at a reasonable price. Next, I checked the e-bay auction site where you can buy practically anything under the sun. I saw, over the space of a week or so, old bikes being sold for £70-£80 and also some newish bikes for £200-£300.

One bike in particular caught my eye. It was an 18 month old Orbit Ventura in pretty good condition with a quality specification. Bidding had already reached £300 with a couple of days left to the end of the auction. I kept track of this bike and at the last moment put in a bid of £450. It wasn't good enough, the bike sold for £477.

Ok, back to the drawing board. Surfed the net again and came across the Evans Cycles website. They were offering a Dawes Galaxy touring bike for £600 post free. The normal retail price was £750 and I'd seen this bike offered for £700 elsewhere. This was an offer I couldn't refuse. Without having seen or ridden the bike, on Sunday 11th February, in a celebratory mood after watching the Wales rugby team defeat Scotland 28 points to 18, I bought a brand new touring bike.

Most people tend to take for granted the many wonderful inventions that are part of our daily lives. My first bike was given to me as a Christmas present a few months after my 9th birthday. It's only recently, though, that I began to wonder about the origins of the bicycle and who invented it.

Leonardo Da Vinci has become famous for his code recently. Some papers of his from the 1490s show sketches of what can only be a bicycle. There is no evidence to show that it was ever made though.

Comte Mede de Sivrac made a wooden scooter-like contraption called a celerifere in France around 1790. The German, Baron von Drais went one better putting handlebars on a similar invention, the Draisiennes, which he exhibited in 1818. Neither had pedals and this type of vehicle was generally known as a velocipede (fast foot) or sometimes the boneshaker.

A Scottish blacksmith, Kirkpatrick MacMillan, made a bike with foot pedals in 1839. It never caught on for some reason.

Around 1870 James Starley, at his Coventry Sewing Machine company, built a bike with a large front wheel and small back wheel - the penny farthing. He also made a tricycle called the Rover which was developed into a two wheeler with a chain. The Rover company later went on to make motorbikes and cars.

H. J. Lawson made the first chain driven bike in Brighton in 1874. It was called the Brighton Dwarf because the wheels had a diameter of only 23 inches. The Birmingham Small Arms company acquired his idea and BSA bikes became very popular in Britain in the early 20th century. Many years ago, my next door neighbour, Bryn, had a BSA bike. I was naïve enough to ask him what the initials stood for. He said, "Bloody Sore Arse".

Evans Cycles promised a delivery time of 5 to 7 days and true to their word my Dawes Galaxy touring bike arrived on February 15th. Unable to contain my excitement, I assembled the bike straight away. A couple of laps up and down the street was enough to convince me that I had bought a bike which was more than adequate for the journey I had planned. It felt light and responsive yet solidly built.

Here, those with a technical mind will relish a chance to read the bike specification. For the rest of you this is the boring bit. The bike has a 53 cm traditional frame with Reynolds 531 tubing. The gears are 27 speed Shimano Deore with bar end shifters. The wheels are made by Shimano with Alivio hubs and stainless steel spokes. Tyres are Continental Country Ride. Stopping power is provided by Tektro Oryx cantilever brakes. The final and most important detail I'll leave to my dear wife who said, "Ooh, it's a nice shade of green, isn't it?"

The following day I proudly rode my new bike down through Cornelly to show it off on the promenade at Porthcawl. This trip was only 13 miles because my running experience has taught me that steady progress is safer than jumping straight in at the deep end. It was also very cold.

With the mode of transport snuggled up safely in the garage it was time to set about planning the route. Originally, I'd thought of taking a train to Chester. When Ian heard this he said, "Don't take the train, Dad, I'll drive you there." The first stage would be accomplished with ease.

I reckoned on taking about 11 or 12 days at about 50 miles per day. After first consulting my athletics fixture list, I settled for the month of June when the days would be at their longest and accommodation would hopefully be easier to book with the kids still in school.

I had thought of taking a tent at one time. You can stop practically anywhere, at any time with a tent. Then I read Josie Dew's book "Slow Coast Home" which made me realize camping was not for me. Her description of freezing, wet nights wrapped in multiple layers of clothing made me shiver. What settled the issue for me was the day she needed a poo while camped in an open field near a busy railway line. Although she was mightily proud of being able to perform the deed into a plastic bag while crouched inside her tent, I thought this is not for me. I need Mr. Crapper's wonderful invention and some privacy. I don't need 5 star luxury, a simple bed and breakfast will do fine.

Starting with Chester I contacted the Baba Guest house because I'd stayed there before with the Harriers. My luck was in, they had a room for June 9th the day before my epic journey was to begin.

The route was only roughly following the coastline and not in and out of every bay and headland. There were some places like Caernarfon, Aberaeron and Carmarthen in which I particularly wanted to stop because I hoped to meet up with friends there. Geraint immediately offered me a bed for the night when I told him I would be passing through his home town, Carmarthen.

The other places were quite quickly booked also, but Tenby became something of a problem. Ivy Bank and Sunny Bank, Kingsbridge and Sea Breezes, even Osnok had no rooms. The main problem was that my itinerary meant staying on a Saturday night in a Tenby which has become famous for its stag and hen party weekends. Eventually, the Hammonds Park Hotel came up trumps. They only had one room left which meant that I had the luxury of a double room all to myself after a night out on the town in Tenby.

During all this booking of rooms there was a vague disquiet at the back of my mind. This was a demanding schedule for someone who'd never done a bike tour before. What if something went wrong? Ever the optimist with my glass half full rather than half empty, I quickly disposed of those thoughts and carried on with the preparations.

While all this planning was going on I was still running a couple of miles a day despite a problem with my left knee. I've learned to live with a troublesome right knee. A specialist told me a few years ago that I had a touch of arthritis which was only to be expected in someone of my age. How easily you can be written off.

It's very frustrating to be injured when you're a keen sportsman. Over the years I've spent a fortune on fees to private physiotherapists. The old NHS system annoyed me greatly because of its pedantry. A visit to the GP would only result in physio treatment after referral to a specialist which could take months. The new hospital in Port Talbot has a physiotherapy department which you can phone direct and get an appointment in a day or two. Common sense has prevailed.

So I had treatment on my left knee. Because I use orthotic insoles for my dropped arches, the physio referred me to a podiatrist to check them out. After a thorough examination, the podiatrist said that my left leg was 8mm shorter than my right leg. My hips, spine and shoulders were all rotated because of this so he put a heel raise in my left shoe.

That evening, after having been sat at my desk for a few hours, I walked into the kitchen to make a cup of tea. As I switched the kettle on I suddenly realized that my left knee was no longer painful. From there on I was able to get back into full training and even the dodgy old right knee felt better.

I continued cycling during this period. Only one day a week, during what was one of the longest cold spells we've had for years. It meant wrapping up well and wearing a pair of plastic bags on my feet sandwiched between two pairs of socks to keep my feet warm.

February started out well for the Welsh rugby team with a win over Scotland. The remainder of the season was a nightmare. It started with the departure of Grand Slam winning coach Mike Ruddock in extraordinary circumstances. Captain, Gareth Thomas, collapsed after an amazing TV interview and didn't play again. Wales then lost badly to Ireland and could only manage to draw with a much improved Italian team.

# *March*

*W*ith only France left to play, I wasn't confident of a win to end the season. As it happened, Wales did lose but played really well and were unlucky in the end. Oh well, there's always next season and, as a postscript, the best coach in Britain, Gareth Jenkins, (entirely my opinion) has been appointed to the national post.

Back on the cycling front, the cold spell continued through March and there were several days when cycling wasn't particularly enjoyable. Cycling 20 miles with ice block toes and streaming eyes and nose isn't much fun. If only Wales, with its wonderful scenery, was 1000 miles further south it would be perfect.

On March 20th, I sold my old GT racing bike. There just wasn't enough room in the garage for 3 bikes, so one had to go. It was advertised on e-bay and was bought by a guy from Yorkshire for the bargain price of £98. He also paid the postage fee.

# *April*

*T*he Meteorological Office has officially classified 1st March as the first day of Spring. It felt anything but spring-like through March, and April started in much the same way with the temperature remaining below average. I continued to cycle once a week, increasing the mileage gradually to a peak of 32 miles.

April 4th was a sad day when I went to Geraint's mother's funeral at Narberth Crematorium. She was 94 years old and had been quite active until the last few months. The sun, however, made a welcome return that day which also happened to be Geraint's birthday.

A cycle tour requires more than just a bike. As the weeks went by I gradually accumulated the remaining equipment, mainly through my favourite shop, e-bay. The list of purchases included a multitool which is the equivalent of a Swiss Army knife for bikes. It has screwdrivers, spanners, socket set, Allen keys and a puncture repair kit all fitted neatly into a custom built pouch.

The bike came with a rear pannier rack fitted, but no front racks. A search on the Dawes website drew a blank. After a few days of surfing the net I discovered that Tortec made front racks which would fit almost any bike. I was then very lucky to buy a used pair on, yes; you've guessed it, e-bay, which I quickly and easily fitted to the bike. There's a huge selection of pannier bags out there, so they were acquired quite easily.

Another piece of equipment which I considered essential was a bike computer. This would enable me to record trip mileage, time, average speed and maximum speed. I'm a bit of an anorak about things like that. I've also kept a running diary ever since I started my athletics "career". At the end of December 2005 I'd run a total of 31,476 miles - $1^1/_4$ times around the world.

I asked if this was the case and when he answered yes, I said of course we would take him into the airport. His name was Ole Jonas Storli, known as Ole Blind, a keyboard musician on his way to Norway to play a concert with his jazz/funk band. He was a remarkable person and I have to admire his will to live life to the full despite his disability.

We returned home from Copenhagen on 2nd June. This meant I only had time for one 40 mile bike ride, sandwiched between two athletics meetings, before the start of my epic journey.

# *Friday, 9th June*

*There was a young man from old Chester*

*Whose wish was to be the court jester*

*But his jokes were so bad*

*That they drove the king mad*

*Now the jester does fester in Leicester.*

On this day in 68 AD the Roman emperor Nero committed suicide; in 1892 songwriter Cole Porter was born and in 1870 novelist Charles Dickens died.

Summer had arrived at long last. Ian was ready to accompany me, his eye having healed remarkably well after the trauma he'd been through. It was hot and sunny as we loaded my bike into the car and set off for Chester at 10.45am with me driving so that Ian would be fresh for the return journey.

We travelled up through the middle of Wales until we reached Newtown where we took a break. Newtown is not so new. It received its charter from Edward I back in 1270. It was built on a bend in the River Severn which has proved over the years to be both a protector from enemies and a destroyer by flooding.

The car park was almost empty. One vehicle which did catch my eye was a red open top Audi with a bald headed man asleep in the driving seat. Briefly discussing his chances of being sunburned, we left him slumbering to cross the suspension footbridge to Dolerw park. In the river below, a huge shoal of tiny fish were sunning themselves in the shallows. After watching them for a few minutes we sat on a bankside bench to eat our sandwiches.

Newtown has two famous sons. Born in 1771, Robert Owen was the founder of the Cooperative Movement. Sir Pryce Pryce-Jones of Dolerw was born in 1834 and founded the world's first mail order business. As we walked back to the car, we noticed that the sleeping slap head had gone. I sincerely hoped that he didn't get sunburned.

The temperature peaked at 29 °C on an otherwise uneventful journey which saw us arrive in Chester at 2.40pm. We pulled into the rear car park of the Baba guest house in Hoole Road to be greeted by the lovely landlady Mrs June Smith. She allowed me to move some plant pots so that my bike could be chained to a steel staple on the rear wall of the house before showing me to room 7. It was a twin-bedded, ground floor room with en-suite shower and spotlessly clean. Co-incidentally, it was the same room I'd had the last time that I stayed at the Baba. If the window was opened I could have climbed straight onto my bike, which was very reassuring. Ian helped me to unpack and then left for home. I was on my own from here on.

The Baba guest house at 65 Hoole Road, Chester was the birthplace in 1917 of Group Captain Geoffrey Leonard Cheshire VC, OM, DSO, DFC, Baron Cheshire of Woodhall. He was a distinguished pilot during WW2, the youngest ever Group Captain at that time and was awarded the Victoria Cross for outstanding courage and determination in the face of the enemy. He also succeeded Guy Gibson as commander of the famous 617 Dambusters Squadron.

After the war he founded Cheshire Homes, a charitable organisation which cares for disabled and terminally ill people. In 1959, he married Sue Ryder who was also the founder of a charity.

After the war, Leonard Cheshire dedicated the rest of his life to the care of the disabled and terminally ill. Cheshire Homes have expanded to almost 60 different countries worldwide. He was made a peer in 1991 and died in July 1992. His Victoria Cross is on display in the Imperial War Museum and in a 2002 poll he was voted 31st in a list of the 100 Greatest Britons. It was an honour to be staying in the birthplace of such a distinguished and selfless man.

***Outside the Baba, Chester***

It's funny how you press the buttons harder on a remote control when you can't get the thing to work. I switched on the TV just to get a weather report for the next day when I realized what I was doing. Sitting on the end of the bed I didn't have quite the right angle. Moving a few feet cured the problem and the forecast was good too.

After a refreshing cup of tea and some biscuits, I set off to look for the Sustrans cycle track. Their website showed that it was a disused railway line which was quite near to Hoole Road. With a map to help it didn't take long to find and would make it a little easier when I set off in the morning.

I then headed into the city centre for some sight seeing. Chester was probably founded by the Romans around 75 AD. The famous England footballer and multimillionaire, Michael Owen, was born in Chester on 14th December, 1979, a birth date which he shares with my son Ian.

Welsh footballer Ian Rush played for Chester in 1979/80 before joining Liverpool and then returning as manager in 2004. In between he also played in Italy about which he is quoted as saying, 'It was like playing in a foreign country'.

The main stand and offices of the Saunders Honda Stadium can be found in Bumpers Lane which is in England. The pitch, however is across the border. Chester play in the English Football League, but it's a case of the green, green grass of home being in Wales.

I entered the city through the Eastgate below its magnificent clock created to celebrate Queen Victoria's diamond jubilee in 1897. Turning right off Eastgate Street, I soon came to the cathedral which is dedicated to the Anglo-Saxon princess St Werburgh who died in 690. There appears to have been a place of worship here since the introduction of Christianity in about 200 AD. The oldest part of the current building is from the Norman period of more than 900 years ago. In its time St. Werburgh has been an abbey and a nunnery. It has been a cathedral since 1541 after Henry VIII's dissolution of the monasteries.

Renowned as a politician, celebrity and wearer of jolly jumpers, Gyles Brandreth was conservative MP for Chester from 1992 to 1997. At the time of writing he holds the record for the world's longest after dinner speech of more than 18 hours. An interesting anagram of his name is "rashly bred gent".

Continuing my walk I turned into Northgate Street and then on to the Town Hall. This imposing red and grey brick building with its spire on top of a tower is Gothic in style. The Irish architect W. H.

Lynn won a competition to design the building which was opened by the Prince of Wales (the future Edward VII) in 1869.

I popped into the tourist information office which is a part of the Town Hall. They had the usual maps and tourist guides and a selection of souvenirs. I've been collecting bookmarks for many years, mainly bought in the places that I've visited. Most of the 240 bookmarks I own have the place name written on them. They range from Venice to Disneyland in California and from Malmo in Sweden to Dunedin in New Zealand. The one I bought in Chester didn't carry the city name. It said Cheshire Cat, above which was the head of a big, ginger tom with a silly grin on its face. It was irresistible.

I sat on a bench in the Town Hall Square to enjoy the late afternoon sunshine. A short distance away, a gentleman of African ancestry was praising the Lord with the words, "The Son of God came, not to be served, but to serve and give up his life for the people". As he moved further down the square he began singing, but I could no longer make out the words. Closer to me, the pigeons were billing and cooing at my feet. I couldn't understand what they were saying either.

After the Romans left, Chester became part of Wales until the Saxons captured it in the 7th century. It is highly likely that their word "caester" for any Roman buildings was corrupted to give Chester its name.

Walking back through Eastgate Street, I turned left at the Cross into Bridge Street. These streets along with Northgate and Watergate are famous for their rows. At ground level, they appear to have normal shop fronts. On the first level above are more shops in a series of continuous covered galleries. These galleries are peculiar to Chester and are the only examples known in the world. The Three Old Arches in Bridge Street dates from the 13th century and is thought to be the oldest surviving shop front in Britain. Most of the remaining galleries are Victorian copies and as such are the oldest known building renovations.

No one really knows why these galleries were built. Some say it was to protect the upper shops from Welsh attacks in the 13th and 14th centuries. Another theory is that the debris from older buildings was pushed back to give street frontage to the shops and the floor level behind then had to be raised. Whatever the reason, these rows give a unique medieval feel to the city centre.

Did you know that it's impossible to lick the tip of your own elbow? No? Neither did I until I met this old gent on the banks of the River Dee. I'd left the city through the Bridge gate then turned left onto the riverside promenade known as The Groves. Here there are steps down to the water, kiosks, pubs and a 19th century band stand. I sat on a bench overlooking the river. In front of me there was a cruise boat called the Lady Diana. A big sign advertising 2 hour river cruises departing at 12.00 noon and 2.30pm meant that I was too late for a trip up the river.

A few minutes later, an old man in an old, grey suit approached and asked if the space next to me was vacant. When I replied yes, he sat down at the other end of the bench. He remained silent for a few moments then remarked on the lovely weather and what a fine city Chester was. I asked if he lived in Chester to which he said, "No, I'm just here on a day trip. I get lonely since my wife died, so I try to get out a bit. It's been almost five years now".

He didn't need much prompting after that. He told me how they'd married when they were both 22 and were looking forward to their 60th anniversary when she fell ill and died. He wasn't a misery guts though. He was as cheerful as anyone in those circumstances could be. Then with a twinkle in his eye, he got up and said, "I have to go now, thanks for listening to an old codger like me. I'll tell you one thing before I go. Did you know that it's impossible to lick the tip of your own elbow?"

Well, have you tried it yet?

As I mentioned earlier, I left the city through the Bridge Gate. Crossing the River Dee here is the Old Bridge which has been here, with only a few alterations, since 1387. Originally built with a drawbridge, it was wide enough to let in friends and also narrow enough for easy defence against enemies. The bridge has seven unequal arches. Upriver, I got a nice photo of the weir built by the first Earl of Chester in 1093. The effect of the weir was to make the water deeper and faster flowing which helped navigation and also powered the water mills built on this north side of the Dee.

***The weir, Chester***

The mills were demolished at the start of the 20th century to be replaced by an hydroelectric plant in 1913. In 1958, this plant was closed to make way for a water pumping station which is still in operation today.

Traffic across the bridge, controlled by lights, is only one way at a time. I happened to notice as I passed the bridge Chester's consideration for its cyclists with an advanced stop line for bikes at the lights.

From The Groves it was only a short walk up the hill to the Roman amphitheatre. Only discovered in 1929, half of it has been partly excavated while the other half has Dee House and the County Court built on top of it.

Most Roman forts had an amphitheatre outside their walls. The Chester amphitheatre is a military type with a smaller seating area than those that served a civil population. This arena would have been used mainly for training soldiers. They were also entertained here with such things as boxing, wrestling, cock fights and bull baiting. Gladiator fights were also common. Criminals, slaves and prisoners' of war of both sexes were forced to fight in the arena. A special fate awaited offenders against the state. They were either tied to a stake or left naked and unarmed to face starving wild animals. Another favourite recreation was to watch animals being hunted down and killed. If there had been any animal rights activists back then they would probably have ended up in the arena as well.

Leaving the amphitheatre, I turned left just before the New Gate into the Roman Gardens. This garden does not date from Roman times, it was established in 1949. It is pleasantly laid out with lawns, Cypress trees, flowers and marble benches where you can sit and contemplate the scene. At the end of the Roman Garden there are steps and a gently sloping pathway for disabled access back to The Groves.

There is a Roman theme to the planting with Rosemary, Thyme, Salvia and Acanthus all of which they were familiar with. There are also Roman artifacts placed in a formal style throughout. The most interesting of these is a hypocaust - Roman central heating. The slab floor of the building was supported by two foot high tile pillars. The heat from a furnace on an exterior wall was conducted under the floor and out through chimneys incorporated into the walls. An ingenious system of underfloor heating, but pity the poor slave who had to feed the wood into the furnace.

As the warm summer evening drew on I began to feel hungry. I returned to the main entrance of the gardens then walked through what is still known as the Newgate even though it was first built in 1553. Walking down Eastgate again, I saw a big blue Rolls Royce car pull up outside the 5 star Grosvenor Hotel. While the concierge was opening the door on the hotel side, the other passenger door on the roadside opened. A very attractive lady of slim build probably in her early forties stepped out. Wearing what looked like a very expensive pale yellow gown with matching high heeled shoes and handbag, she almost fell as her heel went over on the cobbles. I averted my eyes as she quickly looked around to see if anyone had spotted her stumble. When I looked again she was walking elegantly towards the hotel entrance. I smiled and said to myself, "I saw what happened, but your secret is safe with me - and my readers".

Wetherspoon's pubs have a reputation for no frills, good value food and ale. If you've been in one Wetherspoon's then you've been in them all. The pub in Foregate Street was no exception; it followed the usual open plan design. If you want a meal, you first choose a table then give the table number along with your order to the barperson. This is all very well for two or more people. One orders while the others occupy the table. Not so good when you're alone. Having chosen a table I then had to order my meal and hope that someone didn't sit there while I was at the bar. Luckily no one did.

I ordered five bean chilli followed by fruit salad for dessert. Another reason for going to Wetherspoon's is that they cater for vegetarians like me. What is a vegetarian? A professor of Philology at Swansea University once told me that vegetarian was a very ancient Welsh word whose literal meaning is, "He crap hunter". How much truth there is in that, I don't know.

As I sat waiting for my meal I thought about the next day's cycle ride. The weather forecast was good, so I was looking forward to completing the 50 mile journey in good time. Then it hit me. "Oh!", I said, out loud. "I've forgotten my bike computer!" What made me think of it, I don't know, but I knew for certain that I'd left the computer behind. I'd written a check list and had even left it off that. Having left home by car, it hadn't entered my mind. If I'd left on the bike, it would have been the first thing I'd missed. It was too late to do anything about it then.

Feeling a little despondent, I laboured a little over the chilli, which in fairness was quite tasty. While waiting for the dessert, I tried to convince myself that I didn't really need a bike computer. I'd managed without from the age of 9 anyway.

I wasn't the only potty person running the walls at this unseemly hour. Within a couple of minutes a middle aged man coming towards me shouted a cheery good morning to which I replied likewise. Soon after a young woman, also running towards me, (was I doing this wrong?) answered my greeting after a half worried stare in my direction. I met the same woman later on the other side and this time she gave me a more confident smile.

Running alongside Chester Racecourse, the wall almost disappears. This is due to the street level having risen to almost the top of the wall. The race course is known locally as the Roodee. This derives from the Saxon word for cross "rood" and the Norse word "eye" meaning island. Literally then it is the "Island of the Cross". Many centuries ago the water covered this area except for a small island which had a stone cross on it. A remnant of the cross can still be seen in the middle of the racecourse today.

Having completed the two mile circuit of the wall, I went in to Tesco's to buy some sandwiches and fruit for later in the day. Seeing only one young woman at the middle checkout, I went there to pay. Her trolley was full to the brim which meant I had a long wait while dripping sweat all over the floor. Eventually, she paid her £132 bill and I was able to continue my run back to the Baba. Showered, dressed and starving, I enjoyed a good breakfast of Weetabix, fruit juice, tea, toast, scrambled eggs and baked beans.

With my panniers packed, the bike was ready to roll. While settling the account, I asked landlord Bill Smith how long he'd been at the Baba to which he replied, "About 19 years now". I asked, "Did you give this place its name?". "No, it was already a guest house when we bought it and we decided to keep the name." I wondered if he knew the origin of the name. Mr. Smith replied, "One of the previous owners was Moroccan. The word baba is Moroccan for dada or father in English. This was an established business so we kept the name." Mr. Smith then excused himself saying that he had some shopping to do. I jumped on my bike and headed off down Hoole Road again.

Turning right just before the railway station, I joined the cycle track in Brook Lane. This pathway was originally part of the

Manchester, Sheffield and Lincolnshire Railway completed in 1890. It later became the Great Central Railway until it closed to passengers in 1969. Also known as the Mickle Trafford Line, it closed down completely in 1992. It then became the Millennium Cycle Track, the first phase of which opened in June 2000.

This was a pleasant start to my great bike journey. A lovely, sunny morning for whizzing along a flat, traffic free path. With less than three miles under my wheels, I left England and crossed the border into Wonderful Wales.

There were several cyclists and walkers out, most of whom had a cheery greeting for me which I returned. Then I saw something I've never seen before in my life. A young man came towards me wearing a helmet and a figure-hugging ski suit with elbow pads and knee pads. On his feet he had roller blades, in his hands he had rubber ended ski sticks with which he propelled himself along at a fair old rate. He was past me in a jiffy. As a point of interest, did you know that a Jiffy is an actual unit of time? It's equal to $1/100$ of a second. Read on and you will be educated.

There was a bit of a climb up onto the bridge over the A548, then soon after I came to the Hawarden Bridge over the Dee. To allow ships to pass, this bridge has a central section which can be swung open. It's been a long time since a large ship has been this far up river so this function hasn't been used for a few years now.

I cycled straight off the Hawarden Bridge then 200 yards further on turned sharp right and ended up on the platform of Shotton railway station. I turned around and on the way back to the bridge asked a middle-aged man the way to Connah's Quay. He said in a squeaky, scouse accent (a bit like Emlyn Hughes), "You should have turned left off the bridge, then sharp left again to go under it. The cycle path goes under the bridge and that will get you to Connah's Quay". I had expected to turn right after the bridge. With my glasses on, I could then see on the map the left hand loop in the path. A sign at the end of the bridge would have been very useful though.

Connah's Quay developed initially as a port. It is now an industrial centre with three power stations and the Corus Steelworks.

The town probably got its name from a pub called the Old Quay House which was owned by a Mr. Connah. The local Deeside College has high class sports facilities on site including a running track where I competed last year in the Welsh Athletics League. It is also the home of Welsh League soccer club Connah's Quay Nomads.

So far the cycle path had been a boon. In Connah's Quay it just weaved through the streets so I decided to use the direct route on the A548 which led me quite quickly to Flint. In 1277, Edward I started work on the first of his Welsh castles here in Flint on a site overlooking a ford of the Dee. A rocky outcrop below the castle was known by the Old English word flint. It's quite likely that this is how the town got its name.

The road here runs in a north westerly direction from Flint to Prestatyn. It was relatively flat with glimpses of the Dee Estuary on my right as I passed through Bagillt, Greenfield and Glan-Y-Don.

***Duke of Lancaster, Mostyn***

Near the town of Mostyn I thought I was hallucinating. The sea was out of sight , but in the middle of a field on my right was a huge white passenger ship with a black and red funnel. Just to prove that it was real, I stopped to take a photo.

Intrigued by this surprising sight, when I got home I searched the internet, but couldn't find anything about this ship with the little information I had. I was listening to the Roy Noble programme on Radio Wales soon after, when Roy asked his listeners if they had seen anything unusual by the roadside. I sent him the photo of the ship and asked if he could mention it on air. It's thanks to Roy's listeners that the following facts came to light.

Jill from Holyhead said that the ship was used as a restaurant. Bill and Lyn from Mancot said it used to be a market. Wyn Roberts from North Wales said she (the ship) used to sail between Dublin and Holyhead. She was towed to Mostyn to be used as a restaurant and nightclub, but is now used as a warehouse. Mair Jones from Porthcawl said her father sailed on the ship in WWII as a hospital carrier in charge of the morgue. It went over to France on D-Day to pick up the wounded. Thanks once again to all who made the effort to phone in.

The ship is the Duke of Lancaster. She was built by Harland and Wolff in Belfast, who also built the slightly more famous Titanic. She had two sister ships, the Duke of Argyle and the Duke of Rothsay which were passenger only steamers owned by British Rail. They saw service mainly between Heysham and Belfast in the 1950s and 60s. I don't know what's happened to the sister ships, but it's a shame that such a fine ship as the Lancaster lies rotting away in a field in Mostyn while her owners, Solitaire Clothing company of Liverpool use her as a unique warehouse. As an afterthought, why is it that, with such an obviously masculine name as Duke of Lancaster, this ship is still referred to as "she"?

Making good progress I soon entered Prestatyn, one of the oldest seaside resorts in Wales. The Victorians pressed into Prestatyn on the new railway line after 1848 for its healthy sea bathing and clean, fresh air. The current Deputy Prime Minister, John Prescott, was born there as was musician Mike Peters of 'The Alarm'. One of Wales' leading authors, Emyr Humphreys, was also born there in 1919. I've just finished reading one of his novels called 'The Shop' and thoroughly enjoyed it.

As I cycled along Prestatyn's four mile seafront, I passed the tourist information and Offa's Dyke Centre. If I'd turned left here and followed the Offa's Dyke Trail, Chepstow would only have been 177 miles away. I resisted the temptation.

Without quite realizing it, I was soon cycling through Rhyl with its famous Sun Centre. The last time I was in Rhyl was on a rugby tour with Cwmafan RFC in 1969. According to the newspaper headline at the time it was a 'Successful North Wales Tour by Cwmafan'. We lost narrowly 12 points to 8 at Bangor, beat Llandudno 15-0 and the final match was a 9-0 victory over Rhyl.

I have vivid memories of this tour for very good reasons. Firstly for scoring a try in each of the three matches and secondly I spent the last night of the tour in Rhyl Hospital. A blow in the mouth left me concussed and needing four stitches inside my lower lip. I was lucky not to lose any teeth. This was before the days of gum shields. The hospital was full to overflowing, so I had to spend the night in the corridor. Fortunately, they did have a spare bed for me.

Along this stretch of coast it's difficult to know when you've passed from one town to the next. I had to cycle on the pavement to bypass the traffic held up repair work to the Blue Bridge at Kinmel Bay and then I arrived in Towyn. The town has made a remarkable recovery after being flooded during one of the worst storms of the century in 1990.

I cycled on through Abergele which was the site for Britain's first serious rail crash in 1868. Some runaway trucks containing paraffin hit the Irish Mail train resulting in the death of 33 people. A tragedy in today's terms, but unprecedented back then.

Continuing on the A547, the road went up the steepest incline that I'd so far had to cope with. Near the top of this hill I was surprised on looking left to see a steep drop down into a quarry with a small lake at the bottom. The Llanddulas Quarry Company cut limestone blocks from this quarry for many years. Limestone is made of dead sea creatures and shells which have become very hard after being under sedimentary pressure for millions of years. Because of its strength, limestone is used extensively in the construction industry. I took a photo and as I remounted my bike I wondered whether the quarry owners nickname could have been "Rocky".

On again, into Colwyn Bay where I recognised Eirias Park as I cycled by. I've run cross country and also competed on the track there a few times. No time to visit the Mountain Zoo, just keep right on cycling through. No time to visit the privately owned pier either. I remember reading a Western Mail article a few years ago about the sale of the pier. 31 year old Steve Hunt had always wanted to own a pier so he sold his house to buy the Victoria Pier which first opened in 1900. I think he could be throwing money into a bottomless pit. I wish him luck with his huge restoration project. Ex Monty Python, Terry Jones and ex James Bond star, Timothy Dalton were both born in Colwyn Bay.

*Colwyn Bay*

Missed the turning to Rhos on Sea. I was in Mochdre before I realized it. (Mochdre is Pigtown in English. Why it's called that I don't know because I didn't see any there.) I soon hit the A470, though, and followed that right to the seafront in Llandudno. After checking the street map, I soon arrived safely at the Jenivore Hotel in Arvon Avenue.

I was greeted by a young lady with long, black hair dressed casually in a white t-shirt and black slacks who was sitting in the small front garden. She turned out to be the receptionist and she knew my name when I said that I had a reservation. I think she was probably Greek by the sound of her accent. She asked me to leave my bike in the garden while she showed me to my room. It was on the ground floor, so off we went after I'd locked up my bike.

I thought she'd made a mistake when she opened the door at the end of the corridor. The room was accessed through a little, windowless lobby three feet square which was like the Black Hole of Calcutta till she switched on the light.

It would have been a fair sized double bedroom with a bay window except for the addition of an en suite shower room. Along one side wall was a single bed, on the other side was a huge double wardrobe. In the middle of the room were metal framed bunk beds which reminded me of the cell in Ronnie Barker's "Porridge". Lodged in the bay window were two four foot long side tables with a lamp and TV on top and two electric radiators underneath. The only space left was between the single bed and the bunk beds, but they must have thought it a shame to leave it empty so an armchair had been placed there. One of the upper sash windows was open a few inches and must have been so for a few years judging by the paint on it. All my efforts at moving it proved fruitless.

The bedroom door opened on the wrong side. It was stopped at a right angle by the en suite wall and the end of the wardrobe was so close to it that there was only a 15 inch gap to get into the room. There were no tea making facilities and no towels. The one saving feature was that the other door leading off the Black Hole opened into a store room where I was allowed to keep my bike safely and conveniently at hand.

Had a shower, cup of tea and a cereal bar then set out to explore Llandudno. In the corridor, I noticed a linen room with the door wide open. Inside were sheets and towels freshly returned from the laundry. I helped myself to a towel which I took straight back to my room. This was probably just an oversight on the hotel's part.

A short walk brought me to the pier in all its faded glory. It only has some amusement arcades and souvenir shops on it now. From the end of the pier there was a grand view of the Great Orme on one side and on the other the Little Orme and the splendid seafront town of Llandudno. Built in 1877, extended seven years later, it was voted Pier of the Year in 2005.

*Llandudno and Little Orme*

Llandudno is Welsh for St. Tudno's Church. The church lies on the north side of the Great Orme surrounded by a huge cemetery which still serves the town today. St. Tudno lived during the 6th century, but the earliest parts of the church date from the 12th century. It is still a working church and during the summer months open air services are held there every Sunday morning.

The Great Orme is a country park, a site of special scientific interest and an area of conservation. It's home to many different types of plants, butterflies, more than a hundred kinds of birds and a herd of Kashmiri goats.

There are two modes of unusual transport to get you to the top. Opened in 1902, the tramway is the only remaining funicular system left in Britain. The trams are fixed to a cable and can only be stopped and started when the cable stops and starts. The tramway is in two sections, so passengers need to change cars at the Halfway Station. Here you can take a break to visit the Bronze Age Copper Mine Complex.

At the summit terminus you can just step out of the tram and walk straight into the well-equipped Visitor Centre. A short distance away is the Summit Complex which in previous lives has served as a telegraph station, hotel and golf club.

The other transport system is a cabin lift which can be boarded in Happy Valley to take you directly to the Summit Complex. Opened in 1969, it still remains, at just over a mile, the longest single stage cable lift in Britain.

I sat on a bench on the pier between two women who were sitting at opposite ends. The one on my right ignored me, the one on my left acknowledged me with half a smile. She must have been about 50, medium length, dark hair with highlights and of slim build. She wore a white, short sleeved, frilly blouse and loose black trousers.

I hadn't been there long when a young boy came past behind us carrying a balloon. The balloon first hit the lady's head and then hit mine. We looked at each other and laughed. I asked her if she was on holiday. She replied that she lived in Llandudno. We chatted about the merits of the town for a while and then she said, "I love Llandudno, but it nearly cost me my marriage a few years ago. We'd not long moved into Old Road, right on the tramway. I liked it there, but nearly every time the tram went past, the cupboard door in the toilet would open. I kept asking my husband to fix it, but he never did. I got really fed up with it and one day, after he'd gone to work, I phoned a carpenter. Fair play, he was there a couple of hours later.

He couldn't find anything wrong, so he said he'd wait in the toilet till a tram came past. He went inside and shut the door. Soon after, my husband came home from work. He went straight to the toilet before I had a chance to tell him what I'd done. He had a hell of a shock to see the carpenter and asked what he was doing there. The carpenter said to my husband, 'I know you're not going to believe this, but I'm waiting for the tram'".

Walking back through the town, I got my glasses out to read the street map. When I opened the case, one of the arms fell out and the screw that was supposed to hold it in place had disappeared. I was still able to use them, but they were lopsided and liable to slip off my nose. Just a short distance down the road I came upon a Boots Optometrist shop.

The optometrist was a bright young lady with short blonde hair and dressed in a smart, white, medical type of tunic. I asked what time they closed and she said, "Five thirty. What's the problem?" I looked at my watch which showed 5.29. More in hope than expectation, I explained about my glasses and she said, "That's ok, I'll fix that for you now". In two minutes she'd not only repaired the broken arm, but tightened up the good one as well. I thanked her and asked for the bill to which she replied, "That's ok, no charge". I could have kissed her, but settled for a, "Thank you very much, you've been brilliant".

The Victorian's love of seaside resorts led to meticulous planning when they built the town centre. With wide streets, elegant buildings and a two mile promenade known as The Parade, Llandudno has earned the title Queen of Welsh Resorts. I left the 'Queen of Optometrists' to sample the sea air along the prom. Halfway along, I took a seat with the purpose of trying to compose some limericks for this book. I thought Caernarfon was difficult to find rhymes for, but Criccieth was even worse.

Phoned home to give Ad a progress report, then set out in pursuit of my evening meal. I found a nice Italian restaurant called Casanova in Gloddaeth Street. One of my favourite foods is pizza with a nice fresh salad. This is usually what I have for lunch on Saturdays at home. With this thought making me feel even more hungry I climbed the stairs to the restaurant only to be told that they were fully booked.

Disappointed, I walked on until I came to Wetherspoon's which was in the spectacular setting of a former theatre called the Palladium. My experience in the Chester Wetherspoon's had put me off so I passed this one by.

A couple of streets away I was lured like a moth to a light bulb by a distant neon sign which turned out to be Tribells Fish Restaurant in Lloyd Street. When I checked out their menu I found to my delight they served Pizza Vegeteriana so I went straight in and placed my order.

On the next table was an English couple in their late thirties who had two children with them. The youngest looked about a year old while the other one was a boy of about four. This is not a naughty child story, they were both well behaved. It's not much of a story at all really except that the little boy had a stutter. It was unusual in that he didn't get stuck on the first letter of the word like most stutterers. Instead, he repeated the first word of each sentence about four times. I've never heard that before. When asked what he wanted to eat he said, "Can can can, can I have chips, please". I later heard him say to his father, "Will will will, will you cut up my sausage, Daddy?" This happened every time he spoke.

Being so close I couldn't help overhearing that this was their first day in Llandudno, so they were having supper out as a treat. They would be going shopping the following morning to buy food which Mummy would then prepare in their self catering holiday flat.

I enjoyed my pizza salad, paid the bill, and then set off for the Jenivore. On the way back, I bought a bottle of lager in an off-licence. It was an unusual size bottle - 710 mls of Beck's German Beer which I couldn't resist. After I left the shop it dawned on me that it didn't have a screw cap and I didn't have a bottle opener. Luckily, soon after I found a Spar-type shop which sold me the 'Wine Waiter's Friend' for £1.99. This was a combined bottle opener, corkscrew and knife which should come in handy on any future travels.

Back at the hotel, I enjoyed my bottle of Beck's while writing up the journal and went to bed at 10.45pm.

# Sunday, 11<sup>th</sup> June

*There was a young lady from Cemaes*

*Had pleasure and joy as she fed mice*

*One bit her big toe*

*Which angered her so*

*That she cut off the tails of them twice*

On this day in 1184 BC Troy was sacked and burned; in 1910 Jacques Cousteau was born; in 1947 sugar rationing ended in Britain; in 1979 John Wayne died.

Had a fright in the night. Woke with a start and realized when I came around that it had been a clattering, metallic noise. Switching on the light I saw that it was 2.30 am and lying on the floor beside the bed were the hotel keys. I soon realized that I must have left the keys on the bed and kicked them off as I slept. Couldn't get back to sleep for ages after that and was wide awake again by 6.20 am.

Got up then, went through my usual warm up routine before setting off to run around the Great Orme. It was a nice, sunny morning again, ideal for running and cycling. Entered Marine Drive just after the pier, running in an anticlockwise direction with the one way system.

The road was undulating with plenty of climbs to test my stamina. I soon came to the lighthouse which is not itself a tall building. It stands on a cliff 325 feet above the water, though, making it the highest lighthouse in Wales when it was built in 1862. It ceased to function as a light house in 1985 and is now a quirky little guesthouse.

Exactly half way round Marine Drive is the Rest and be Thankful Café. I was thankful to be half way round, but didn't need a rest. Neither did I stop for a drink at the Ffynon Gaseg (Mare's Well) a little further on. The song says, "Keep on Running" which I did, past the site of the Royal Artillery School and the executive houses of Llys Helig. The last half mile back to the West Shore was all down hill. This isn't as easy as it sounds. Each footfall is lower than the previous one and your foot hits the ground with greater force. With my dodgy knees, I prefer to run uphill.

I noticed as I ran that marks had been painted in white on the road every 100m all the way around. I think the last one was at 7800m, but I'm not sure. It took me 50 minutes to get back to the Jenivore so I reckon I ran about six miles in total.

I got a much different impression of the hotel in the morning. The restaurant was freshly decorated, the tables had immaculate red cloths and the cutlery was good quality stainless steel and spotlessly clean. The staff were efficient, attentive and pleasantly polite. I enjoyed an excellent breakfast of fruit juice, cereal, baked beans on toast, all washed down with a nice pot of tea. I also helped myself to an apple and a banana from the fruit bowl on the way out. I bought some sandwiches from the Londis shop around the corner, packed them on the bike and left Llandudno at about 9.00 am.

I rode down Gloddaeth Street which is a wide avenue. Despite this, there was a car in front of me which was going so slowly I had to free wheel. He eventually accelerated away after a few moments. I was pretty pleased about that because, as The Great Philosopher said, "Man who cycle behind car soon get exhausted".

My route then followed the A546 into the town of Conwy with its magnificent castle. Not built to the usual Norman concentric plan, it has eight huge towers placed where the underlying rock formation allowed them. Edward I must have urgently needed this castle because it was completed, along with the town walls in only four years between 1283 and 1287. An impressive and striking sight as I cycled across the River Conwy.

As well as having one of the biggest castles in Europe, Conwy can boast of having the smallest house in Britain. Measuring just 1.8m wide by 3.05m high it does have an upstairs bedroom overlooking the quayside. The last owner was 6foot 3inches tall Robert Jones who couldn't stand upright in his tiny home. It would probably be described by an estate agent as a desirable one up/one down property with fantastic views of the Conwy Estuary.

Just outside Conwy I spotted a sign for cycleway5. Crossing a bridge over the A55, another sign told me to turn left which I did. I knew there was something wrong immediately, especially when a cyclist coming from the opposite direction shouted and pointed to the other side of the road where he was. I realized then that the cycle track was on the pavement and I'd been heading down the slip road for the A55 into the flow of traffic. Luckily there was no traffic and I moved as rapidly as my loaded bike allowed onto the cycle track.

The going was pretty good on this trail and it eventually moved away from the main road to take its own course along the seashore. At Penmaenmawr, I had a feeling something was wrong again when the tarmac ended without warning and became a rough, stony path. I turned back to where some men were working on their yachts. I asked one of them if he knew how I could get back to the cycle path. He said, "The path ends here". Then, pointing to a huge, looping flyover almost above our heads, he said, "If you go up there, turn right at the top of the hill in Penmaenmawr, that road will take you back to the cycle track, but watch out for the traffic as you cross the main road". He also said that there were plans to extend the cycle track through in the future although that didn't help me then. A sign at this point would have been handy.

After passing through PMM, I came back to the A55. Here, I had to dismount to gallop  across four lanes of thundering traffic before finding the cycle path again. West bound vehicles enter a tunnel here,

I had to go over the big rock. At the other end of the tunnel I had to run another gauntlet of speeding traffic, This time, though, it was only two lanes as the track came down into the middle of the dual carriageway.

There is a two foot wide strip of tarmac between the gutter and the solid white line along the edge of the roadway. This was my cycle path on the A55 until I left at junction 11 to join the A5 to Bangor.

With pangs of hunger gnawing at me, I stopped at what I thought was a park. It turned out to be Bangor Crematorium, but the well manicured lawns provided a pleasant setting for a peaceful, picnic lunch. There was absolutely no trouble from the other occupants either. As I set off again, the song 'Didn't we have a luvverly trip the day we went to Bangor' came into my head and stayed there for the rest of the day.

Bangor is one of the smallest cities in Britain yet boasts what is probably the longest High Street in Wales. The city has a cathedral, university and singers Aled Jones and Bryn Terfel were born there. Welsh Rugby international wing Dewi Bebb was also born in Bangor.

The last time I was in Bangor was for the Welsh Intercounties Cross Country Championship. There were races for all age groups in male and female categories. A coach full of runners left Swansea early on the morning of the competition. As the journey progressed, team manager Gerry Batty, realized that we might be late for the first race. The under 14 girls had to change on the bus and warm up by running up and down the aisle till we arrived in Bangor. Unfortunately, their race had already started, but they were allowed to join the under 16 race just to give them a run after travelling all that way. Such are the trials of amateur athletics. I sat by Gerry on the bus for a short while. He had recently been given a t-shirt which had written on it, 'I'm in the bomb squad, if you see me running try to keep up'.

Cycled on through Bangor until, quite suddenly, there was the Menai Suspension Bridge. I couldn't pass over it without taking a photo which a few other people were also doing at the same time. Ireland joined the United Kingdom in 1800 resulting in an increase of traffic for the Holyhead ferries. It was then deemed necessary to build a bridge across the dangerous waters of the Straits. It took Thomas Telford more than six years to build his suspension bridge which had to be high enough to allow the tall ships to sail below. Completed in January 1826, it was the biggest suspension bridge in the world at that time.

*Menai Bridge*

I've never crossed the Menai Straits before, so I felt quite excited as I rode off the bridge and turned right for Beaumaris. The name Beaumaris means 'Beautiful Marsh' which it was when good old Edward started building his castle there in 1295. To me it has rather a stunted look, especially in comparison with Conwy and Caernarfon castles. This is probably because the money and materials ran out before the walls had reached their planned height.

**Beaumaris**

I couldn't find any road signs in Beaumaris, so I asked a young man for directions. He was exceedingly helpful and soon I was peddling off to Pentraeth. The only thing he didn't tell me about was the very steep hill just up the road. I had to get off and push the last 50m to the top. This was the first time I'd been forced to dismount on a hill in the whole of my life. With five loaded bags on the bike it wasn't the last time either.

Passed on through Pentraeth, then just after Benllech I spotted a bench beside  the road. Here I had my Sunday lunch of cheese and tomato sandwiches with a banana as dessert. I was reluctant to move on. The bench must have been deliberately sighted here for the magnificent view through a metal-bar gate across the cow filled fields to the sea.

*Sunday lunch break, Benllech, Anglesey*

Back on the A5025, I didn't stop to see the picturesque port of Moelfre with its all weather lifeboat called 'Robert and Violet'. The boat was paid for with an anonymous donation. I don't know why its got two names, perhaps I should have contacted the Roy Noble programme again.

Parys Mountain, during the 1800s, was the major supplier of copper to the known world. A local miner called Robert Puw was happy to accept a bottle of whiskey and free accommodation for life in exchange for the mining rights. He wasn't the first to find copper in Parys, there is evidence that the site was mined as far back as the Bronze Age and also during the Roman period. Did you know that two unnamed men from Cardiganshire are credited with inventing copper wire after a prolonged tug of war over a penny.

With a mountain of copper only a few miles away, it was inevitable that the port of Amlwch would be significantly developed.

It was also recognised as an important shipbuilding centre, largely due to the expertise of a local man called Captain William Thomas whose streamlined schooners sailed all over the world in the late 1800s.

The mining of copper on a large scale ended many years ago and the port of Amlwch caters mainly for the tourist trade now. Anglesey Tall Ships, owned by Robin James, is one company which operates from the port. Mr. James owns two schooners, the Pickle and the Cymru. The Pickle is built like the Mimosa, the vessel that took the first Welsh settlers to Patatgonia in 1865. Mr. James plans to recreate the voyage of the Mimosa for which, as I write, he is looking for a crew of ten people to accompany him on a 12 week round trip in the autumn of 2006. The voyage will be filmed for television and will provide anyone with a nautical leaning a wonderful opportunity to sail a tall ship on an historic journey.

Leaving Amlwch behind, I was soon approaching the town of Cemaes Bay where I'd booked a room for the night at Pentregof guest house. Their travel directions state that you should go past the village of Cemaes and the Brookside garage and, 'at the top of the hill on your right is Pentregof'. After a day of ups and downs this very last hill was nearly the one that broke the camel's back. It was almost as steep as the Pentraeth hill, but I was determined not to let it beat me. I pedalled right to the top and Pentregof was a most welcome sight as I rode into the courtyard.

I was welcomed at the door by owner Chris with the immortal words, "Oh, I didn't expect you to be on a bike!" However, he had catered for cyclists before. Around the side of the house he'd constructed a triangular bike shelter which was open ended, but covered over with canvas. After unpacking, he showed me to a pleasant single bedded room with ensuite which was clean and cheerful with a view across the fields to the sea.

In the other direction, behind Pentregof, is the Wylfa Power Station which opened in 1971. It has two Magnox reactors and four turbine generators. Even though Wylfa provides over 40% of Wales' electricity it will not be feasible to meet refurbishment costs and it will close down in 2010. There are the green campaigners who welcome the closure. There are also many people who will lose their jobs and the economy of Anglesey will suffer. Whether to build a Wylfa B power plant is currently under discussion.

I left Llandudno at 9.00am and arrived 53 miles later in Cemaes Bay thoroughly knackered. I stripped off, took a shower while the kettle boiled, then had a cup of tea and a cereal bar. Then I had another cup of tea and another cereal bar and an apple.

Feeling a lot better, it was time to explore Cemaes Bay. I asked Chris how far it was to the town and if I could get a meal there. He replied, "It's a fair walk, and it's not much of a town, more of a village really. There won't be any shops open on a Sunday evening, but try the Woburn Hill Hotel. They're open every day and you'll have a nice meal there".

It was all downhill to the sea, so I walked, if necessary, I could get a taxi back up. I strolled down the High Street to the pretty harbour and beach, then out along the quay. The tide was out, so only the little river Wygr rippled past the old stone pier which was completed in 1835.

I walked out along the west beach where a young lady was throwing a stick for her lively, black Labrador to chase. Then I ambled back to the end of the pier where I watched some children playing in the shallows. The beach here shelves very gently making it safe for bathing.

It was a very pleasant, sunny evening so I sat on the pier to phone home. I'd just finished my chat with Ad and was about to leave when a middle aged man with two mongrel dogs walked by and said hello. He wore a white t-shirt, black track suit bottoms and had a baseball cap on his head.

On his way back, he stopped to remark on the good weather then went on to tell me about the time he used to sail his own boat out of Cemaes. Then he said, "I remember once, a few years back, this bloke put in to Cemaes because he was having problems with his boat. It was a nice little Sea Hawk and his wife and teenage son were on board. They lived in Manchester, but he'd always wanted a boat and this was the first time he'd taken her out. He said she was very sluggish and not being an expert asked if I could help. I checked everything I could think of, but there was nothing obviously wrong. I suggested waiting for the tide to go out so that we could check the bottom of the boat. We went up to the Harbour Hotel and a couple of hours later went back to the pier. The tide had gone out and the problem was obvious. The boat was still attached to its trailer."

**Cemaes Bay, Anglesey**

At the top of the High Street is the Woburn Hill Hotel. I entered the restaurant which was empty, but went through to the conservatory where six or seven people were already dining. The walls were bedecked with plastic fish, butterflies, boats, birds and vines. Nevertheless, it had a homely feel and I was made to feel welcome as I was shown to my table.

From a good choice of vegetarian meals, I ordered the broccoli bake which was excellent. There was a couple on the opposite table who looked to be in their early 60s. They were friendly and from their accent I guessed they were from Birmingham. They corrected me in no uncertain terms by saying they were from Wolverhampton. The man was quite tall, overweight and had greying hair and a beard that was almost white. By the way, did you know that the word 'almost' is the longest word in the English language with all the letters in alphabetical order, unless someone knows different. His wife was average build with curly hair and glasses.

The guy told me he was a road tanker driver and his wife worked night shifts in a factory. He said, "We love Anglesey. We've been coming here once or twice a year for the last twenty years". I told them about my cycle ride and about my running.

The driver said, "I used to run a lot in my younger days. I don't run anymore now though, as you can see", pointing to his paunch. "I've run two marathons, both in three hours thirty minutes. I used to enjoy running till I got too old for it." I told him that you're never too old to run.

He then said, "I've got other interests as well. I enjoy bird watching and I love birds of prey in particular. A couple of years ago I had a great birthday present from my missus. It was a day at a hawking centre where I got to handle the birds as well. I really enjoyed that and I'd love to get a bird of my own."

They went on to give me tips about Anglesey and a list of must-see places which I thanked them for. All too soon they finished their meal and I was sorry to see them go.

I'd finished my meal as well by then. There's not a lot to do in a small place like Cemaes Bay on a Sunday night the waitress said. The only alternatives are eating and sex, so I settled for a really delicious chocolate fudge pudding in a puddle of cream.

Having had enough to eat, it was too early to go to bed so I left the restaurant to have a drink in the bar. Over a pint of Stella with a Jamieson's whiskey chaser I spent an entertaining hour listening to the conversation between the hosts, Brian and Kath, and a middle aged couple. The man was heavily built, had a bald head and was clean shaven. His lady was tall, slim, had long, straight, blonde hair and was expensively dressed, but in an almost tarty way. She had also overdone the make up in my opinion.

Baldy was from Cemaes originally. He said his father had died a few years ago. His mother had then sold the house, but, wanting to stay independent, had moved into a caravan in his sister's garden. He also had two brothers with whom he'd fallen out and never saw now. He'd recently been divorced from his wife of 29 years. The woman he was with was his girlfriend. He'd also recently retired from his job as a Hertz hire car rep at Manchester airport.

Finishing my drinks, I asked for the bill which totalled £21.70. When Brian, the landlord, handed me the visa receipt it had been rounded down to £21.00. I thanked him for a nice meal and for his hospitality before leaving. It was such a lovely evening that I walked back up to Pentregof. I was glad I did because I saw a beautiful red and gold sunset over Wylfa. I wrote up my journal and was in bed by 10.40pm.

# Monday, 12th June

*There was a young man from Caernarfon*

*Who always went out with his scarf on*

*He forgot it one day*

*And in bed had to stay*

*Until his hot fever was far gone*

On this day in 1849 L. P. Haslett patented the gas mask; in 1897 Carl Elsener patented a pen knife later known as the Swiss army knife; in 1942 Anne Frank had a diary for her 13th birthday; in 1964 Nelson Mandela was jailed for life; in 1965 the Beatles were awarded the MBE.

I woke quite early to the sound of heavy rain pattering against the window pane. This is not the sort of wake up call I like, so I turned over and went back to sleep. At 7.00am it was still raining quite heavily. It's not often that I take a day off running, this was one of those days because I felt quite stiff and tired after yesterday's exertions. There was still a long way to go on this journey yet.

At 8.00am I was the only person in the dining room and had Chris' undivided attention. I breakfasted well on Weetabix, scrambled egg on toast with tomatoes and mushrooms followed by a pot of tea and more toast with marmalade.

Chris was very sociable. In between serving the food he stayed and chatted with me. He said, "I've had a few jobs in my time. I was the manager of an abattoir in my early days. I didn't like that much so I left and joined an insurance firm in Shropshire".

After over twenty years in the insurance business he grew to hate that too. "I got really sick of it because the company's first move was always to try to get out of paying any claims. If the customer made a fuss, then they usually paid up. If you mentioned the ombudsman, then payment was virtually guaranteed."

He retired from the insurance firm and had been at Pentregof for seven years. "The idea was that it would be a part time B+B, mainly busy in the summer with not much happening through the winter. It didn't work out like that. The place is rarely empty because we regularly get workers from Wylfa staying here".

I couldn't buy any sandwiches in Cemaes so I asked Chris if he could make me some. He came back from the kitchen with a neatly wrapped pack containing not only sandwiches, but a banana, a packet of crisps and a paper serviette as well. When I asked the price of the packed lunch Chris insisted that there was no charge. I thanked him for his generosity and to cap it all it had stopped raining as well.

From the top of the hill at Pentregof it looked bright towards the south as I mounted my trusty steed for the journey ahead. I was determined to complete this trip no matter what the weather. However much you criticise it, the weather will take absolutely no notice anyway.

After Tregele, there were only Llans to be seen on all the signposts till I got to the A55. Llanfechell, Llanfairynghornwy, Llanrhyddlad, Llanfaethlu, Llanddeusant, Llanfwrog, Llanfachraeth and, last but not least, Llanynghenedl. Please pause for applause if you managed to read that lot without twisting your tongue.

There wasn't much traffic on the A55 and I was soon cycling into the centre of Holyhead. It's the biggest town in the county although it isn't actually on Anglesey, it's on Holy Island. There have been settlements here since prehistoric times. This was the site of the only three walled Roman fort in Europe. The fourth wall was the sea.

Holyhead is famous as a ferry port with links to Dublin and Dun Laoghaire.

The breakwater, completed in 1876, is almost two miles long. More than seven million tonnes of stone were used to build it at a cost of £1.29 million and 40 lives lost.

The comedienne, Dawn French was born in Holyhead in 1957. One of the ferry companies operating out of the port is B+I. An American tourist was once heard to ask where he could find the B plus one ferry.

The South Stack lighthouse is a sight I've always wanted to see. It was easy to find, but not so easy to cycle to. The lighthouse was built in 1809 on a little island known as South Stack Rock. There was no bridge until 1828. The only way of getting across before that was in a basket on a rope after descending more than 400 steps down the cliff. Now the lighthouse is automated and has no keeper.

In the car park, I said hello to a man who looked about 65 years old. He was wearing a checked jacket, jeans and had a good head of thick white hair. His accent sounded rather strange. I asked him where he was from to which he replied, "Morecambe originally, but Formby now. I've spent most of my life in America though. I left England in my teens, had a few different jobs early on, then became a lighthouse keeper".

I can't remember which lighthouse, but he went on to say, "I was a keeper for more than 20 years, then they automated the lighthouse. It became a museum, so I stayed on to be the visitor guide".

We chatted about his experiences, then he said, "I remember a woman coming into the lighthouse one day looking pale and agitated. She said she had a confession to make and took an old notebook out of her bag. She said a couple of years before, on an impulse, she'd taken the book as a sort of souvenir. I hadn't noticed it had gone because there were a lot of old books on the shelves there. She told me that ever since she'd taken the book, she'd suffered a series of misfortunes. Nothing really serious. A cracked windscreen on her car, a water leak flooded the kitchen, breaking a coffee pot.

The last straw was when she was burgled. The thief had taken money and jewellery, but the strange thing was he'd left the notebook lying on its own on the table. She knew then that she had to take the book back to where it belonged."

"I found out later that the book was owned by a keeper who'd spent his whole working life at the lighthouse and he'd died there in the late 1800s. The woman sent me a letter just before I left America. She said that it had been a year since she'd returned the book and she'd had no more accidents at all."

The ride back down from South Stack was really exhilarating. I was back in Holyhead in no time. I took the B4545 for Trearddur Bay where Tracey Morris was born in 1968. Tracey, now living in Leeds, was the first Welsh (and British) woman to finish the London Marathon in 2004. This qualified her to run for GB in the Olympic marathon in Athens later that year where she finished 29th in 2hours 41minutes. A very creditable performance in very hot and humid conditions.

I sat on a brick wall just after Trearddur to have a tea break. They're a fit lot in this place. Two cyclists, a walker and two runners came past while I sat there. They're friendly as well, they all said hello. The two runners, a man and a woman, were probably members of Cybi Striders. The man was about 45 and running comfortably. The woman, perhaps a little younger, was struggling, but being encouraged by her partner.

The land was quite flat here which made it an easy ride to the A5 which runs parallel with the A55. There was very little traffic, so it was almost like an outsize cycle track. Above me though, there was a constant roar of low flying aircraft. Nearby RAF Valley was opened in 1941 to defend Belfast, Liverpool and ships in the Irish Sea. Today, it is the home of No.4 Flying Training School, the Search and Rescue Training Unit and the Mountain Rescue Service.

William Jones was born on a farm near the village of Llanfihangel on Anglesey in 1675. He was a distinguished mathematician who also taught navigation and maths on board ship during a short naval career. Pi is the ratio of the circumference of a circle to the diameter. Pi is constant at 3.142 (3 decimal places) for every circle. In 1706, William Jones was the first to use the Greek symbol *TT* to represent this constant and it has been used internationally ever since. This did not make William big headed because he was a very Pi-ous man.

It did cross my mind to turn right on to the A4080 through Aberffraw and Newborough down to the Britannia Bridge. The A5, my cycling motorway, was such easy going that I decided to stick with it.

It's strange that as I write this the news is dominated by the death of Sir Kyffin Williams. He was born in Llangefni in 1918 just a short distance off the A5 on which I was travelling. He had to leave the army in 1941 because he was epileptic. The doctor advised him to take up art which he did with great success. He was probably the greatest Welsh painter of his time. He was renowned as a portrait painter which he regarded as his main work. He was also inspired by the landscape and farming communities of his beloved North Wales.

A member of the Royal Academy, Kyffin believed in 'real' art and was exasperated by some of the works which won the Turner Prize. He famously said it was like, "awarding the championship in the Welsh Black Cattle class to a sheep" of one winning entry. He was a hugely popular character who has made a massive contribution to the cultural heritage of Wales.

On the coast south west of Newborough (with all the Llans on Anglesey, where on earth did this name come from?!) there is a place called Llanddwyn Island. This is a misnomer really, it's an island only at the highest of tides.

There's a legend attached to this place which is named after the 5th century princess Dwynwen. The daughter of King Brychan, Dwynwen fell in love with Maelon. Her father wanted her to marry someone else which she was unwilling to do. Somehow, Maelon was turned into a block of ice so Dwynwen asked God for these three wishes, that Maelon be restored, all true lovers should find happiness and that she should never be married.

These wishes came true and Dwynwen became a nun on Llanddwyn Island where she soon became known as the patron saint of lovers. Many people made a pilgrimage to her holy well where the fish could give a sign as to the faithfulness of a lover. St. Dwynwen's Day is on 25th January and she is our Welsh equivalent of St. Valentine. Some time ago I was moved to write a poem about Dwynwen:

*With twenty four daughters the king was blessed*
*Of these fair Dwynwen was by far the best*
*To Maelon Dafrodill she gave her heart*
*But father's judgement sundered them apart*

*No marriage to Maelon for sad princess*
*To God she turned in her cheerlessness*
*An angel appeared from paradise*
*Turned master Maelon to a block of ice*

*But God took pity and with wishes three*
*Saved poor Dwynwen from her misery*
*Maelon was thawed and to him she stayed true*
*Unwedded was Dwynwen her whole life through*

*For an island refuge Dwynwen now sought*
*Devotion to God was her only thought*
*She built there a church in order to praise*
*And sing to the Lord the rest of her days*

Perhaps I should stick to limericks in future. I won't be writing one about Llanfairpwllgwyngyllgogerychwyrndrobwllllantysiliogogogoch which is where I stopped to eat the lunch that Chris from Pentregof had packed for me. The name means the church of Saint Mary in the hollow of white hazel near the rapid whirlpool at Saint Tysilio's church near the red cave. I didn't see a hollow of white hazel, a whirlpool nor a red cave as I passed through. Rumour has it that this name was made up as a tourist gimmick when the railway station opened in 1848. A little further on, I almost hit the pavement trying to get a look up at the column with a statue of the first Marquis of Anglesey on top. Then there was the Britannia Bridge.

When plans to take the railway through to Holyhead were discussed, it was realized that the Menai Bridge was not strong enough to carry the extra weight. Robert Stephenson designed and built the Britannia Bridge which opened in March 1850.

The increase in traffic and a fire in 1970 led to proposals that the bridge should be rebuilt in two tier form with a roadway on top. It was this roadway which I used when I left Anglesey with plans to return one day.

Crossing the bridge was a hair-raising experience. There was a strong crosswind blowing which made cycling difficult. At each of the arches, the wind speed increased, decreased as I passed under, then increased again on the other side making it very difficult to control the bike. It was with some relief that I stopped on the far side of the bridge to take a photo. I made it safely across, but then a rhyme came into my mind about what could have happened. It goes like this:

*I got on my bike and went for a hike*

*To the furthermost parts of the land*

*I got a flat tyre, my saddle caught fire*

*Then I fell off and cut my right hand*

With only six miles to go to Caernarfon, I thought I had it sown up. Shortly after joining the A487, there was a monstrous climb that just went on and on. Even after I'd climbed the steepest part, it didn't level off for about another half a mile. This section was dual carriageway, then the last couple of miles into Caernarfon was a very busy single carriageway with occasional glimpses of the Menai Strait and Anglesey on my right.

I had a map and directions for Church Street from the Tegfan guest house website and they were spot on. I found it without any difficulty. It was a big, old terraced house which has been renovated to a high standard.

I was welcomed by Phil, the manager, who was in his 40s, a bit overweight, no airs and graces and a good sense of humour. The owner, whose name escapes me, was very obliging. He told me to cycle around to the lane at the back of the house where he was waiting for me. He showed me into a large storeroom which was rather cluttered, but with enough space for my bike.

Phil then showed me to what was a huge family room with a double bed and a single bed. No en suite, but the refurbishment of the ablution room had only been completed the previous week. There were two showers and two toilets all with locking doors. The first thing I did was to shower. It was strange to step out of the shower (fully clothed mind) to see a young lady (also fully clothed) going into the next shower. I've never been camping or caravanning, so I'm not used to these communal facilities. Back to my room then for a cup of tea and a snack.

Caernarfon is probably the most impressive of Edward I's castles. Building began in 1283 of what was intended to be the English seat of power in North Wales. The nine polygonal towers and banded masonry indicate that this was a special place. The first English Prince of Wales, later to become Edward II, was born in Caernarfon castle in 1284. Charles, the current Prince of Wales, was invested with his title there in 1969.

There was a Morrison's store only a quarter of a mile from Tegfan. On the way there I passed the new Galeri Arts centre. It's a modern wood, glass and metal building opened in April 2005 by Bryn Terfel. I don't know when Morrison's was opened, but they had a good selection of fruit and packed sandwiches.

Took my purchases back to Tegfan and put the sandwiches on the edge of the open window to keep them cool. I then went out to find the Black Boy pub where I'd arranged to meet Hefin Elis. I've known Hefin since 1965 when we met through our mutual friendship with Geraint Griffiths. We played in a band with the unlikely name of the Dream Time People. The band never played a gig, but we had some fun for a while until we all went on our different roads in life. Hefin went on to be a founder- member of top Welsh groups Edward H. Dafis and Injaroc. He has also had a successful career in the music and television industries. The last time we met was in 1966.

The Black Boy was only in the next street. It was too early for my meeting with Hefin so I returned to Tegfan to phone home, you've got to keep your better half happy. We don't argue much, but I've heard it said that the only way to get the last word in with a woman is to say sorry. I can go one better than that. I always get the last two words in - as long as they're, "Yes, dear".

Returned to the Black Boy fifteen minutes early to make sure I wouldn't be late, although a few minutes wouldn't have made much difference after a wait of 40 years. While I was waiting for Hefin, I had a look around the lounge. The room was a decent size with a low, timbered ceiling. The furniture was crammed in as tightly as possible. No two tables and no two chairs were alike. In the corner where I sat was a large, wooden bardic chair with the three feathers insignia carved on the back.

At one end there was a copper canopy over a stove and at the other end a shelf above the seats with some quite large porcelain figures on it. Over the bar was a collection of beer mats yellowed with age and cigarette smoke. Every cross beam in the ceiling had foreign currency banknotes stuck to it. On a shelf behind the bar was a foot high 'doll's house' model of the pub.

Just after I got there, a group of seven Japanese men walked in accompanied by a Welsh woman guide. Two of them spoke reasonable English. When asked what they wanted one of them said, "Welsh beer". They didn't understand pint or half when asked. The barmaid then said, "Large beer or small beer?" The first answer was, "Small", then he said, "Please show me - uuuuuh - cup". By this time everyone in the room was watching and listening. The barmaid showed them a pint glass, "Big" and a half, "Small". The Jap's reply, "Aaah - big" was greeted by laughter all round. They moved across to the restaurant with their big glasses of beer and then Hefin arrived. His hair was greying and I'm sure he won't mind me saying that he'd gained a few pounds since the last time we'd met, but he was immediately recognisable as soon as he walked in. We shook hands and greeted each other warmly. I then invited him to take the big, carved chair while I went to the bar.

With Hefin's permission I switched on a tape recorder then asked him how long he'd lived in Caernarfon to which he replied, "I came here in 1985, so about 21 years".

JD: "How does it compare to Port Talbot?".

HE: "The Welsh language is obviously a lot stronger here than in Port Talbot and the industries have run down here tremendously. In the 60s, this was a fairly wealthy town and people would travel here to do their shopping. With the opening of the A55, people bypass here, they go further afield now. There is some regeneration. There's an arts centre, the Galeri. Things are picking up, but there's too much outside town. They're moving the surgery, the dentist, the pharmacy out of the centre. They're being replaced by charity shops. I don't know if that's the same in Port Talbot?"

JD: "Yes, it's a similar story with us. What's the latest with your TV company now?"

HE: "It was formed in 1992 as Tonfedd, then we amalgamated with Eryri in 1998, became Tonfedd-Eryri. We were doing light entertainment, comedy etc and they were doing dramas so we brought the two genres together. We're joining forces with another company to make an even bigger one, Tonfedd-Eryri-

Cwmni Da. We're working on a new name for the amalgamated company."

JD: "What's your job with this company?"

HE: "One of the directors, with responsibility for light entertainment, comedy and music".

JD: "You've come a long way from Ponty".

HE: "Well yes. That was a good grounding I suppose. The Ysgol Gymraeg with Alwyn Samuel and music and I'm sure we had a few laughs there, so the comedy comes from there. Could be".

JD: "Do you play or sing in a band now?"

HE: "No, very rare. I certainly don't sing. Only backing vocals if I have to. I've never enjoyed singing. In a choir, something like that, fine. But not as a soloist. Played guitar and keyboard. I've been playing bass lately. Filling in really. With Dafydd Iwan, I played keyboard, guitar or bass depending on who was available. I played on some records for Sain when they needed to bring session musicians in. I've enjoyed playing bass more than anything. I wish I'd done it all along.

I've got a collection of guitars, but I don't play them. I've got a Gibson SG, Les Paul, Fender Telecaster, Strat, Rickenbacker, Yamaha acoustic, Aria bass and I've just bought another bass, a Washburn acoustic bass. My house looks musical, but there's not much going on there".

JD: "How long have you been married now?"

HE: "Actually, 25 years coming up next month. My wife, Marian, is from the Welshpool area, Llanfaircaereinion. She was at university in Bangor when I worked for Sain. We met in the Globe pub where the students used to congregate. We've got two girls, one is 21 and the other is 20. The eldest has just finished in Bangor and done rather well. The other one has just finished her second year in Cardiff."

JD: "What's the best thing about living in Caernarfon?"

HE: "That you can live your life in the medium of Welsh. This is one of the few places where, for the largest body of people, Welsh is the first language. It's just a natural way of life. To me, that's the best thing".

JD: "What's the worst thing about Caernarfon?"

HE: "The town needs sprucing up I think. A bit of regeneration. If we had a few stalls, shops, a chain store to bring the people in to spend the money here and not go on the bypass to places like Chester. Parking is a problem here, people want the convenience of going to the supermarket and parking is the main appeal. You can't do that in the centre of old towns can you?"

JD: "Are you still a Welsh Nationalist?"

HE: "You could say that, yes. I have been since my teens, I suppose".

JD: "Has Welsh always been your first language?"

HE: "Not when I was in Sandfields really. The only Welsh I spoke then was at home. All my friends were non Welsh speaking. They all turned to English because of peer pressure in our teens, even Geraint, but we reverted when he came back to Wales.

JD: "Have you ever thought of going in to politics?"

HE: "I'm not the type of person really. I'm not extrovert enough. I haven't got the confidence to speak on that stage or in front of the camera. I'm very interested in politics from the sidelines or reading about it. Or I wouldn't mind writing some articles possibly, but not as an orator".

JD: "Have you worked for Plaid Cymru?"

HE: "Only on election days. Not in an official capacity".

JD: "What about the Welsh Language Society?"

HE: "Yes, one of the campaigners, but I didn't hold an office at all. When the elections come round I help with the canvassing, but that's it really".

JD: "Did you enjoy playing in Edward H?"

HE: "It was a hobby in a band which was popular. It was enjoyable watching the punters enjoying themselves and buying the records. It's nice to look back on. There's been lots of pressure put on us to reform. I prefer to leave the past in the past to be honest. We've done a few special one-offs".

JD: "What about the future?"

HE: "Work? I don't plan to retire yet. The amalgamated company is taking a lot of time. It's a competitive, cutthroat business. All production companies are fighting for a slice of the same cake, balancing finances, not making something too cheap, trying to keep some quality in our programmes".

"I won't be retiring to Spain. I don't like the sun too much. I enjoy winter more than summer actually and it coincides with the football and rugby seasons as well. I've got a season ticket in Anfield. I'm an avid Liverpool supporter. I remember their football in the 70s and 80s. It was superb, head and shoulders above everyone else. They just seemed to take their success in a modest way as opposed to some clubs who tended to blow their own trumpets, too loudly for my liking. I hope that Liverpool can get back to that level and they'll have that dignity in success as well as defeat. I used to play a bit myself in Port Talbot. Once I went to college I did nothing there. Aberystwyth was my downfall".

JD: "What degree did you get in Aber?"

HE: "Welsh. I went in to do music, but I changed after the first year. They expected you to be in a choir or orchestra and learn two instruments. That was far too much hard work. That year Prince Charles was in Aberystwyth, the investiture year. They expected us to take part in concerts to entertain him. I didn't take part which didn't go down very well. I've got nothing against him personally, just the title. He's not our prince, certainly not mine".

Hefin had a meeting to go to, so our time together ran out there. His final comment was, "It was nice seeing you again, John. I'll cycle down to Port Talbot next year to visit you."

It was a pleasure meeting Hefin again after such a long time. He's still the nice, modest guy I knew all those years ago. Playing in the most successful Welsh pop group and being a company director hasn't changed him at all.

I was starving when Hefin left so I stayed in the Black Boy and enjoyed a delicious vegetable chilli. There was a huge choice of food on the menu, not like when I was young and living at home. My mother only gave me two choices - take it or leave it.

Feeling rather full, I took a stroll around the town and down to the seafront just as the stars were coming out over Anglesey. Bed at 10.30pm.

# Tuesday, 13<sup>th</sup> June

*There was a young lady from Criccieth*

*Whose heart for her love would beat quickieth*

*But the young man who moved her*

*Just pretended he wooed her*

*He was really just taking the mickieth*

On this day in 1865 poet W. B. Yeats was born; in 1910 public campaigner Mary Whitehouse was born; in 1920 the USA postal service ruled that children should not be sent by parcel post; in 1970 'The Long and Winding Road' was the Beatles last number 1 song.

Rose at 6.15am to another sunny morning. Went through my warm up routine then set off to run back down the A487 which was fairly quiet at that time of the morning. Ran at an easy pace for the first five minutes, then ran fast for two lampposts and slow for four lampposts. Turned around after 16 minutes and repeated the process on the way back.

The dining room was empty when I went down for breakfast at 0800. Two young ladies came in about ten minutes later. Phil, the manager/cook/ bottle washer served up an excellent breakfast of fruit juice, Weetabix, scrambled egg with tomatoes, mushrooms, beans and quorn sausage. He's quite an extrovert character who huffed and puffed when he was busy, but did a very good job.

The two young ladies sounded American. I just caught snippets of their conversation during which it transpired that they were actually Canadian. They discussed the merits of various breakfast foods for a while. One of them said that her grandfather had had cornflakes and coffee for breakfast every day of his life. He was now 95 and still going strong. Maybe I'll try cornflakes for breakfast tomorrow, I thought.

While I packed my panniers, Phil told me he'd done a fair bit of cycling including a charity ride from Wrexham to Cardiff. He'd also been a semi professional footballer back in his native Liverpool until his knees gave out.

We then said goodbye, but I was to meet him again far sooner than I expected. I rode down the lane and as soon as I entered Church Street I realized that I'd left my helmet behind. I stopped outside the front door, went in and said, "Hello again", much to Phil's surprise, collected my helmet and was on my way.

About five miles later I realised I'd forgotten something else - the sandwiches I'd left to keep cool overnight in the window. It was too far to go back, so if you're reading this, Phil, you're welcome to those sandwiches.

The road was fairly easy going until I turned on to the B4417 for Nefyn. Then there was a climb which got steeper until I had to get off and push. When I reached the crest of the hill, I stopped to admire the scenery and to take a photo. I looked back down the road to see a cyclist riding up towards me. He was in his twenties, riding a lightweight racing bike and pumping powerfully. As he pedalled past I shouted, "Well done, keep it going". In a Yorkshire accent he replied, "It's easy for me, you're all loaded up". He actually had enough breath left to talk as well.

Just above Morfa Nefyn there was a layby with a nice grass bank where I sat to eat some oat biscuits and a nectarine washed down with a flask of tea. Nefyn was made a free borough as long ago as 1355. The town's coat of arms bears three herrings showing the importance of fishing to its past economy. These days Nefyn's main income is from tourism.

Just as I was about to continue, a car came around the corner. The driver didn't seem to be aware of me, so I thought just because he's on the road it doesn't mean his mind is. I waited until he'd passed before setting off. An uneventful ride through rolling hills eventually brought me down to the delightful little seaside town of Aberdaron.

*The intrepid cyclist at Aberdaron*

The poet-priest, R. S. Thomas was vicar of St. Hywyn's church in Aberdaron from 1967 to 1978. Thomas was born in Cardiff on 28th March, 1913 to English speaking parents. He started learning Welsh when he was 27, but was never able to write poetry in his beloved native language. His early poems painted a bleak picture of life in the rural areas where he preached. His later work reached an almost metaphysical level. He was viewed by many as a typical grumpy old man with a reputation for being taciturn and a loner. RS worked with the RSPB and supported the CND. He was a fervent Welsh Nationalist to the point that he refused to support Plaid Cymru because he felt they didn't do enough for Wales.

His name was simply Ronald Thomas at birth. He added the Stuart himself when he was still quite young. One wonders whether Ron Thomas would have been quite as famous a poet as RS Thomas was. If you read any one of the 1500 poems that he wrote, you'll know that he was a very fine writer.

A row of OAPs sat on the promenade, if it can be called by such a grand name, enjoying the view and the fresh sea air. I wanted a photo of me and the bike on the prom as a souvenir of Aberdaron. Being reluctant to disturb the old folks, I hung around in the hope that someone would walk by. After five minutes I gave up and asked the nearest old gent if he'd kindly take my photo. He must have been at least 85 with a white flat cap on his head, grey flannel trousers and a pale blue, hoodless windcheater jacket.

He struggled up from his chair with great difficulty, which made me sorry I'd asked him then. His mind was agile though. He got the hang of the camera straight away and asked me what I wanted in the picture. He did a great job because when the film was developed later the photo came out exactly as I'd wanted.

We talked for a few minutes and he told me he'd been a gardener all his life. He'd worked mostly at a country house whose name I can't remember. He then said, "I still remember the day I got the job like it was yesterday. Two of us went for interview and being poor, both of us went in the only clothes we had. The other gardener was a bit older than me, full of himself and a good talker. I was very shy so I thought I had no chance.

After the interviews, the colonel called me back in and said I'd got the job. I was really pleased, I can tell you. But I was puzzled as well, so I asked him what had swayed it my way. He said that when he looked at my trousers I had patches on my knees. When the other man left the room, he had patches on his seat.

It was time to leave Aberdaron. I'd planned to use the coast road and not seeing a sign asked a painter working on a nearby house if the road we were on would take me to Llanbedrog. He said, "Yes it will, but no, you can't go to Llanbedrog that way". Puzzled, I showed him the map and he became even more confused, giving me directions I couldn't understand.

Pointing to Rhiw on the map, I said, "According to this map the road we're standing on will take me to Rhiw". To which he replied, "There's been a landslide at Rhiw, the road's collapsed". That was why the road went to Llanbedrog, but didn't. I thanked him for his help and mounted my bike. As I did so, he asked, "Are you Dutch or German?" I said, "No. I'm from Port Talbot in South Wales". The painter said, "Oh are you. Because we get a lot of them around here". I said thanks and goodbye once more. His final word was, "Sorry", which made up for everything. He had saved me a wasted journey on the road to Rhiw and back after all.

As I was pushing my bike up the steep hill out of Aberdaron, I saw an old corrugated tin shed by the side of the road. On closer inspection it turned out to be the Islyn Bakery. Having left my sandwiches in Caernarfon, I popped in and bought a cheese and potato pastie, a packet of crisps and a piece of bara brith cake. Not food for dieters, but plenty of carbohydrates for a long distance cyclist.

About a mile out of Aberdaron, a great weariness came over me. I pulled over for a rest, a cereal bar and a drink of water. This revived me quite quickly and I was off again. The route was very hilly with high hedges on both sides of the road. I kept going until 1.40pm when I spotted an unlocked gate leading to a nice, grassy field. I checked that there was no resident bull, then sat in the field to eat my goodies from the bakery with a very pleasant rural scene set out before me.

Back on the road, there was a nice long downhill stretch into Llanbedrog where I joined the A499 coast road. It wasn't long before I arrived in Llyn's unofficial capital, Pwllheli.

Albert Evans-Jones was born in Pwllheli in 1895. Using the bardic name, Cynan, he won the crown three times and the chair once at the Eisteddfod. He was also elected Archdruid twice. His poem, Mab y Bwthyn (Son of the Cottage), became the most widely read and quoted of Welsh poems in the middle of the 20th century. He was knighted as Sir Cynan Evans-Jones in 1969 and died in 1970.

To most English speakers, though, the name Pwllheli is more synonymous with the Butlin's holiday camp. The camp opened in March 1947 with the motto "Remember, when it's wet it's fine at Butlin's". No one was ever bored on a Butlin's holiday. Their daily entertainment programme had something for everyone. Snooker, table tennis, the glamorous grandmother competition and top acts like Jimmy Tarbuck, Des O'Connor and Dave Allen. The kids had Punch and Judy, pantomime and the Butlin's Beaver Club amongst a host of other things. Ringo Starr appeared with Rory Storm and the Hurricanes at Pwllheli in 1960 before he made it big time with the Beatles. In 1997, Butlin's became a Haven Holidays flagship caravan park known as Hafan y Mor.

The Great Philosopher said, 'Trust in God, but lock up your bike when you leave it'. That's exactly what I did when I stopped at the Lloyd George museum in Llanystumdwy. I pushed my bike up the slope through the very tall, but quite narrow wrought iron gates at the entrance. Just inside, on the left, was a metal railing with a mountain bike chained to one side. I chained my bike to the other side.

Inside the museum, I was greeted by a tall, thin, gangly young man with short, dark hair and glasses. In a classical North Wales accent he asked me for £3 and gave me a brief explanation of what I could see at the museum. It was well worth the money.

There were some fascinating things on display like Lloyd George's baby grand piano, medals, clothes, walking sticks and even a copy of the Treaty of Versailles. In one corner was the 'Lloyd George Crown'. No, he was never king. This was a five shilling piece owned by Thomas Thomas, the first person in Wales to be paid old age pension in 1911. There was also a short documentary film with commentary by Welsh actor Philip Madoc.

A short walk away was Highgate, Lloyd George's childhood home after his father died. He and his mother lived there with his uncle

Richard Lloyd who was a shoemaker. The house and workshop have been sympathetically restored to look like they would have at that time.

*Grave of Lloyd George, Llanystumdwy*

Another short walk through a matching set of iron gates brings you to Lloyd George's grave which was designed by Sir Clough Williams Ellis. It's an unusual grave overlooking the Dwyfor river and is a fitting monument to this great man.

David Lloyd George rose from poverty to Prime Minister, the only Welshman to reach this office. He was known as the 'Welsh Wizard' and Winston Churchill said that, 'The greater part of our fortunes in war and peace were shaped by this one man'. He was internationally acclaimed and will forever be remembered as one of the most skilled politicians in British history.

When it comes to the Welsh language, I'm a bit like a Llansant sheepdog - I can understand it, but I can't speak it. What I should say is that I can understand most of what's said in the South Wales dialect. The North Wales dialect I have great difficulty with.

I mention this because when I stopped in Criccieth's High Street the two gents I asked for directions were speaking in the wonderful words of the Welsh Language, which I couldn't understand. They politely indicated in English how I could get to Marine Terrace where I'd booked accommodation at Awel Mor.

Judith, the landlady, was an attractive well-proportioned woman with short, fair hair and probably in her middle 30s. She was very friendly and made me feel at home straight away. She said I could store my bike in the laundry room at the back of the house and was waiting at the open door when I rode around to the back lane.

When I booked the room, I opted for a sea view with private facilities across the landing. I was glad when I saw the view. To my left was the castle and in front, I could see right across Tremadog Bay towards Harlech, even though it was a bit misty by then.

The room was small, but very clean and well maintained with some nice feminine touches like a single flower in a tall, slim vase. After a shower and the by now usual cereal bar, fruit and tea, I set off for the town.

Criccieth castle has one of the most spectacular sites of any of the Welsh castles. Sitting on top of a rocky promontory jutting out majestically into the sea, it couldn't be bettered by a Hollywood film set. The history of the castle is a bit sketchy with no clear record of when it was built except it might have been in the early 13th century. The castle has a sound strategic position with easy access to the sea. From the top of the towers on a sunny day the coastline of Llyn, Snowdonia and even Harlech castle can be seen.

From the castle I walked along Lon Felin past the lifeboat house where an Atlantic 75 rigid inflatable lifeboat is stationed. The boat has to be transported across the road and a short distance down the shore to be launched into the sea. All was quiet when I passed by, but three days later the crew rescued a swimmer who'd gone out too far and was clinging for dear life to a buoy.

At the top of Mona Terrace, I had to cross what was probably the major influence on the development of Criccieth town - the railway. It arrived in 1868 allowing the Victorians, with their fresh air and sea fetish, easy access to another seaside centre.

I don't know why, but as I crossed the railway a piece of advice that Tarzan once gave Jane popped into my mind. He said, 'Never insult a crocodile before you cross the river'. Which is good advice for anybody.

I checked out the restaurants on High Street and decided that the Bryn Hir Arms had the best choice of vegetarian meals. Further along there was a garage/Londis store where I bought sandwiches for the next day's journey. Turning left a little further on again, I went down West Parade and across the Green to the seafront where I found a coastal path which looked like a good traffic free route for running on. Back in Awel Mor, I sat on the large window sill looking out over the bay while I phoned home.

The Bistro Bach at the Bryn Hir Arms is a small room downstairs with only six tables. When I arrived there was a foursome already there. They all looked about the same age as me roughly. There was only one waitress who was young, had long, black hair and was very attractive. She wore a rather low cut black top, black mini skirt and a wide, white studded belt. She did her job efficiently, but wouldn't win any prizes for charm, she didn't smile once. I ordered ricotta and spinach cannelloni with a jacket potato which was pretty good.

From their accents, the foursome was made up of a north English couple and a Scottish couple. They chatted away about Portmeirion and some of the other places they'd seen on their holiday. Later on the conversation turned to illnesses and medication. The English lady had a louder voice than the others so I couldn't help overhearing as she told the others about her friend Cynthia's headaches. She said,

"Cynthia's husband, Brian, came to bed one night feeling frisky, but she told him not tonight, Brian, I've got a headache. A couple of nights later, Brian felt frisky again, but got the same reply - not tonight, Brian, I've got a headache. A week later, Cynthia went up to bed and Brian came in with a glass of water and two aspirins and said, 'Here you are then, Cynthia.' Cynthia said, 'What's that for?' Brian said, 'Your headache.' Cynthia said, 'But I haven't got a headache.'

When they left, the Scotsman went first and tried to leave the bistro through the storeroom door. The other three were highly amused at his embarrassment, and so was I.

On the way back, I bought a 660ml bottle of Stella. It's thirsty work writing up a journal. They seem to have a thing about odd sized bottles in North Wales. I was tucked up in bed by 10.30pm and was lulled to sleep by the sighing sound of the sea on the shingle below the bedroom window.

# Wednesday, 14<sup>th</sup> June

*A young man from old Aberdyfi*
*Once fancied himself as a luvvie*
*He effected great airs*
*To get people's stares*
*And was famed as the luvvie from Dyfi*

On this day in 1847 Bunsen patented his Burner; in 1919 Alcock and Brown made the first non stop transatlantic flight from Newfoundland to Galway; in 1938 the first Superman comic was published; in 1950 the current Archbishop of Canterbury, Rowan Williams, was born; in 1982 the Falklands war ended.

Got up at 6.20am, opened the curtains to see the sun already shining brightly over Tremadog Bay. Put on my running kit, warmed up, then headed off down the coastal path at a steady pace. When I reached the River Dwyfor, it was too deep to cross. It looked like a different river to the one I'd seen at Llanystumdwy yesterday. Below Lloyd George's grave it was a chattering, cheery brook rushing over the rocks in its hurry to get to the sea. At the estuary, it was a wide, winding, sluggish stream almost too tired to cross the sands.

I ran inland for about a quarter of a mile until the path petered out. I retraced my steps, then on past Awel Mor to the bottom of the castle hill, turned round and ran back to the Green. Walked back to Awel Mor to get my breath back and to cool down a bit. Glancing towards the beach, I saw a white haired lady, who must have been 70, swimming in the sea. I hope I'm as active as her when I'm 70.

Showered and dressed, then took the non essentials down to pack on the bike. Had an excellent breakfast of fruit, muesli, scrambled egg with tomatoes and mushrooms followed by a pot of tea with wholemeal granary toast.

My romantic mind associates Judith and her husband Martin with being the English equivalent of Romeo and Juliet - she's from Yorkshire and he's from Lancashire. Or is it the other way round? Anyway, they have a nine year old son whose voice I could hear coming from the kitchen while I ate breakfast. I heard him ask his dad, "Why have flowers got petals, Dad?" There was an inaudible reply. Then, "Well why have they got leaves then?" Another inaudible reply.

Martin then served up my toast and I said, "Giving you a hard time is he?" Martin replied, "He likes to help out in the kitchen. He usually gets sidetracked onto something else though." I asked if he was going to school and Martin said, "Yes, I'll be taking him in soon. No more awkward questions then. He's doing quite well at school though."

A short ride brought me to Porthmadog. It was named after Prince Madoc or possibly after local entrepreneur William Maddocks. In 1808, Maddocks started work on the Cob, an embankment which enclosed the Glaslyn estuary. By 1825, Maddocks had also built the harbour through which thousands of tons of Welsh slate passed to all parts of the world. In the late 1800s, there was a decline in the slate and shipping industries. The railway arrived in 1867 and the people of Porthmadog had to earn a living from the tourists which it brought. The Ffestiniog Railway, which used to bring the slate from Blaenau Ffestiniog 13 miles away, still operates as a tourist attraction now.

Maddocks had not one, but two towns named after him. He was largely responsible for the founding of nearby Tremadog as well. T.

E. Lawrence, better known as Lawrence of Arabia, was born in Tremadog in1888. Did you know that the film, Lawrence of Arabia, is the only Oscar winning film in which no women spoke?

It was released in 1962, won seven Oscars and the only female in it was a camel called Gladys. I rode out of Porthmadog along the Cob which has a traffic free cycle path and a fantastic view across the estuary towards Snowdonia.

***Harlech Point***

Portmeirion was made famous by the 1967 TV series, The Prisoner. I first visited Portmeirion a few years ago while on holiday in North Wales. It is a masterpiece of fine buildings set out in such a way as to complement the landscape and not crowd it.

Sir Clough Williams-Ellis was born in Northamptonshire in 1883. With very little formal training, he proved to be an outstanding architect. Portmeirion first opened in 1926. Sir Clough continued to add new buildings until 1972.

The traffic came to a halt at temporary lights in Penrhyndeudraeth. The car in front of me had a sticker in the back windscreen which read, 'If they don't have chocolate in heaven, I'm not going'. I wondered if it was being driven by my wife. It wasn't of course, although the driver was a woman. The name Penrhyndeudraeth in English means Promontory of Two Beaches.

I took the toll road here, saving me an eight mile round trip around the estuary. It's a single lane road for most of its length. Running alongside is the Cambrian railway, both using a wooden bridge to cross the River Dwyryd. The 40p toll was only applicable to motor vehicles. Me and my bike passed through for free. To my right was a stunning seascape with Portmeirion perched on its hillside. On the left, a little further on, was a lovely landscape with cows in a field and strange, humpbacked hills behind. This view, however, was spoiled by huge electricity pylons running through it.

Soon after, I turned right onto the A496. This road is flat and I flew through to Harlech, frightening a few rabbits on the way. It's funny how they always run in front of you for 25 yards before sidestepping into the hedge. Our old 'friend', Edward I, began building Harlech castle in 1283. Perched on a platform of rock 200 feet high with the sea at its base then, it seemed to have an impregnable position. It did withstand a siege in 1294, but fell to Owain Glyndwr ten years later before being retaken by the English in 1408.

Harlech was a Lancastrian stronghold during the Wars of the Roses. Until it was captured by the Yorkists after a seven year siege begun in 1460. The song, 'Men of Harlech', famously sung in the film 'Zulu', was written many years later to honour the Lancastrians who held out for so long.

A childish song I remember from my very early days was sung to the tune of 'Men of Harlech'. The silly lyrics sounded something like this :-

*I'm the man who came from Scotland*

*Shooting peas at a nanny goat's bottom*

*I'm the man who came from Scotland*

*Shooting peas away.*

The railway line runs diagonally across the road below the castle. I was lucky to get a few minutes rest while a train negotiated the level crossing because there was a tough climb out of Harlech. It was a case of gritted teeth and lacerated lungs by the time I reached the top without stopping. I'd got my breath back by the time I arrived in Llanfair two miles down the road. Just above the village are the Chwarel Hen slate caverns. Over 100 years ago, the slate from this site roofed a great number of buildings all over Britain.

Made good progress to Dyffryn Ardudwy where those of you with an interest in ancient history would be able to visit a pair of well preserved burial chambers. If you're not interested in history then you could cross the road for some sunbathing on Morfa Dyffryn beach. Be warned though, it's popular with the naturists and on sunny, summer weekends, there can be hundreds of bathers in the buff down there.

With the sun shining and a good road, I enjoyed the ride down into Barmouth. Here, I took a break on the promenade looking out over the Mawddach Estuary. I shared my oat biscuits with a friendly pigeon who'd got in ahead of the usually more aggressive seagulls.

Barmouth's story is not a long one. It was a ship building centre and port until the rise of Porthmadog in the 1840s. It now relies largely on tourism. There is an interesting connection with the Titanic. On board when she sank in 1912 was 5th officer Harold Lowe who was from Barmouth. He survived the disaster, returning in a lifeboat to the sinking ship to look for survivors. In the recent award winning film, Ioan Gruffydd played the part of Harold Lowe.

As I sat enjoying the splendid view, the soporific sunshine and a cup of tea, a party of 10 year old schoolchildren walked past led by two teachers. There's always one, isn't there? My bike was leaning against the harbour railings just in front of me. One of the boys stepped out of line, leaned over the handlebars and tried out the brakes. He gave me a wicked grin before rejoining the line and disappearing into the distance. What can you say? There was no harm done, so I said nothing and had a little laugh to myself.

Barmouth is the starting point for one of the most unusual multi terrain races in Britain. The idea came from two local doctors, Myrfyn Jones and Rob Haworth. Teams of three sailors and two runners have to sail to Fort William in Scotland, stopping to run up Snowden, Scafell Pike and Ben Nevis on the way. Pretty simple then. I've run up Snowden once. I caught the train back down. I'd only just recovered from a knee injury at the time. Well, that's my excuse anyway.

When planning my route, I hadn't realized that the Barmouth railway bridge was open to pedestrians and cyclists. It meant I had an easier day with 10 less miles to cycle. I walked down to the toll booth where a very nice man who could have been Idris Novello Pugh's brother (you'll have to watch the film Grand Slam to get that) was graciously pleased to accept my 70p toll.

The wooden planks of the bridge made it a bumpy crossing. I made it without a mishap and was relieved to find a public toilet a couple of hundred yards down the road. With no one in sight, I took a risk and left the bike outside unlocked. It would have been a long walk home if it had been stolen, but to my relief, it was still there when I came out. My friend, Dai, married his wife in a toilet. It was a marriage of convenience.

The Fairbourne Railway opened in 1895 using horse drawn trams. It was built by Arthur McDougall who owned the famous flour firm. It's only a two mile narrow gauge track running from Fairbourne to Penrhyn Point on the south side of the estuary. Before the Cambrian Railway came, you could catch a ferry from Penrhyn to Barmouth. The ferry only runs in the summer months now.

Inland from Fairbourne is the myth covered mountain of Cader Idris. It is 2927 feet tall, with several legends attached to its massive Ordovician rocks. Sometimes called Arthur's Seat, it seems unlikely that it has any connection with King Arthur and his Knights of the Round Table despite the stories.

Cader Idris translates as The Chair of Idris. The legend says that Idris, a giant who lived on the mountain, got angry one day. He kicked three rocks off the slopes which can still be seen near the foot of the mountain today. Another story says that Idris was a great Welsh warrior who was killed in battle when the Saxons invaded in the 7th century.

As much as I enjoy writing and as poor as my poetry is, I will definitely not be testing out this final myth. Anyone who is brave enough to spend the night on top of Cader Idris will wake up either mad or an accomplished poet or dead.

The town of Tywyn was invaded during WWII. Not by the enemy, but by the British forces. The army used the local beaches to practise landing techniques and some of the D-Day forces were trained there. Nowadays, you're more likely to see windsurfers on the beach. They should watch out for the groynes that cross part of it though.

The Dysynni Cycling Club is based in Tywyn. Only founded in 2001, the club already has almost 100 members and has organised the successful Sea Front Cycle Races for the last three years.

The old slate story is continued in Tywyn. The Talyllyn Railway carried slate from the Bryn Eglwys quarry to Tywyn from 1865 to 1947. In 1950, talyllyn became the world's first preserved railway thanks to a band of amateur enthusiasts.

Since 1983, the local Rotary Club has organised an event in conjunction with Talyllyn called 'Race the Train'. As the name suggests, runners have to race the train from Tywyn to Abergynolwyn and back over a mixture of roads, tracks and fields. The total distance is about 14.8 miles, depending on local farmers. The train has actually been beaten many times.

In the early days of radio, the Marconi Wireless Company constructed a receiving station to the south of Tywyn. In 1918, Marconi sailed into Aberdyfi in his yacht, Elettra, in order to inspect the Tywyn station. In those days, messages were sent by the Morse Code. An anagram of 'The Morse Code' is - 'Here come dots'.

It was only a short, easy ride to Aberdyfi, my next overnight stop. Aberdyfi is a small town with one main street facing the miles of golden sands and the estuary of the Dyfi river. It has a top class golf course and caters for all types of water sports.

Leaning my bike against the railings outside Awel y Mor in Bodfor Terrace, I walked up the four steps to the front door where landlord Brian Johnson greeted me warmly. He told me to take my bike around the back where I chained it underneath the steps of a galvanised fire escape. I went in through the kitchen and followed Brian downstairs to room 2 in the basement.

A room with a view in Awel Mor, Criccieth, one day and a room in a basement in Awel Y Mor in Aberdyfi the next. Having said that, it was a big en suite room with a double bed which was actually a bed settee. The pillows were set between the big, bulky arms of the settee and turned out to be ideal for resting my journal on in bed.

There was a bay window with a double glazed door in the middle. This gave me my own private access and a second escape route should there be a fire; which there wasn't. From the bed I could only see from the knee down the people walking past outside.

There were only half a dozen people enjoying the late afternoon sunshine on the beach in front of Awel Y Mor. Thoughts of Aberafan Beach flashed into my mind as I gazed across the sloping sands. On a sunny day during the miners fortnight back in the 1950s and 60s, daytrippers would descend on Aberafan in their thousands. If you didn't get to the beach early, you wouldn't find a place to put your towel; and not a German in sight.

Young bathers used to go into the sea and not be able to find their parents when they came out. It got so bad that the council painted large white letters on the sea wall above the beach. My Mam always made sure that I knew the letter on the wall before I went down to the water.

It doesn't seem that long ago when we didn't have electricity in our house in Cwmafan. We had gas lights downstairs and candle light upstairs. Even when electricity came along in 1953, there seemed to be frequent power cuts, so we always had a stock of candles in the house. I still keep some candles in the cupboard now.

I remember when I was about 10, my mother was peggi        (I can't believe this coincidence - we've just had a power cut as I'm writing this! That's why I've left the unfinished word above. It's where the power cut happened, honestly. See if you can guess what the word is.)

To continue - I remember when I was about 10, my mother was pegging (did you get it?) clothes on the line in the back garden. I was looking for something in the cupboard and had the bag of candles in my hand. In those days, front doors were always open and neighbours just shouted hello and walked in. Bryn next door did this and, startled, I turned around and dropped the candles in a sink full of water. I said to Bryn, "What am I going to do now, Bryn. The candles are soaking?" His reply was, "No problem, John bach. Just put them in a baking tin in the oven on gas mark 5 and they'll be dry in no time." Which is what I did.

Happy days. I got a slap for melting the candles and Bryn got away scot free. And so back to the beach at Aberdyfi. I walked as far as the jetty where a sign told me that it was 'reserved for the sole use of outward bound'. In 1941, Kurt Hahn and Lawrence Holt established a Sea School at Aberdyfi to prepare young men for the rigours of life on the ocean. This was the first Outward Bound program in Britain. The training has moved on with the times since then, but Aberdyfi remains an important Outward Bound centre to this day.

I used the last film in my camera on the jetty and the chemist didn't stock APS films. He suggested I try the Londis store a few doors down. The lady in Londis was very helpful. I'd bought the old film in Copenhagen and they didn't have that make. She opened a Kodak carton so that I could check the cartridge inside. It was the right one. I bought it and some sandwiches then walked to the eastern edge of the town.

On the way back, I called in to the Victoria Rose gift shop on the off chance that they sold book markers. They had none with the town's name on, but I did buy a nice Victorian facsimile with multi coloured moths on it. And so back to Awel Y Mor to make my daily report home to Ad.

Next on the agenda was the evening meal. I'd checked out the eating places earlier and decided on the Britannia Inn. The Sea View Terrace Bar upstairs had a wonderful sea view. I ordered the penne pasta and a pint of lager and as there were no seats left outside on the terrace, I sat inside facing the window.

The pub had models of sailing ships on all the window sills. One of them (ship not sill) had a definite list to port and didn't look at all seaworthy, even if it was only a model. In the estuary below me, a fleet of small boats reflected the light of the setting sun. A long, lean rowing boat, sculled swiftly by a crew of four, soon disappeared out to sea. On the hill opposite, the rotors of a wind farm remained motionless in the windless warmth of the evening.

Then I heard the dulcet tones of a South Wales accent, "Shall we eat here then, butt? It looks alright, don't it?" The answer was, "Ay, ok butt". Then a loud, "Come on then, girls. Let's sit over here". I turned around to see that there were actually three couples of about my age or a little older settling themselves at the corner table behind me.

From overheard snippets of conversation, it became obvious the men had been playing in a golf tournament. When I got the chance, I asked where they were from. "Methyr" one of them said, "Are you from there too?" I told him I was from Port Talbot so he asked what I was doing in Aberdyfi. He was flabbergasted when I told him about my cycle tour. He couldn't understand why anyone would want to cycle so far.

He mentioned the golf tournament and said that one of his friends, Lyn Mittel, had played last year. He said, "Lyn I call him because we were in the same class in school. Owen Money his name is now. Do you know him?" I said, "Well I don't know him, but I know who you mean and I listen to him on the radio". He asked where I was staying and it turned out that one of the couples was staying in Awel Y Mor as well.

Our conversation petered out and the Merthyr mob started chatting about previous holidays. One of the men told a tale of a trip to America. He said, "We went on holiday to Florida with Robert and Meg. She's always washing clothes, even on holiday. I phoned Meg and asked her in an American accent if she was washing clothes up there because the meter for their room was whizzing around. She took it all in. She said she was sorry and wouldn't wash any more. I told her she'd have to save some water now. The best way to save it was to shower with her husband. She said she would and I had to put the phone down so she wouldn't hear me laughing. Of course, when she told Robert he knew it was me straight away and we had a good laugh about it."

"They got me back though. On the last day, a letter was pushed under our door. It said we owed $30 for telephone calls. It was on official hotel paper as well. I was tamping I can tell you. I took it to the manager and told him how annoyed I was because I'd only made one call. The manager said he knew nothing about it and then I realized I'd been had."

While this was going on, I had a huge portion of  home made apple crumble with cream which was almost as good as Mam's. I finished off the night with a lager and a Jamieson's Whiskey chaser after my Merthyr mates left. Back at Awel Y Mor I updated the journal and was in bed by 10.45pm.

# Thursday, 15ᵗʰ June

*A lady from fair Aberaeron*

*Was fishing one day in the Aeron*

*She caught a big trout*

*And also the gout*

*Then had to stay home with the fire'on*

On this day in 1215 King John put his seal to the Magna Carta; in 1911 Reverend Wilbert Vere Awdry (Thomas the Tank Engine) was born; in 1946 musician Noddy Holder was born; in 1956 John Lennon and Paul McCartney met for the first time.

Got up at 6.20am to be greeted by the sun shining brightly over Cardigan Bay. Put on my kit and went through my running warm up ritual. Jogged across to the prom where the only other person out was a litter picking, ginger haired, council workman. I stood on the shore listening intently in the hope of hearing the famed Bells of Aberdyfi.

There is a legend that says this part of the coast was once many miles wider and protected from the sea by a dyke. Known as the Lowland Hundred, it formed part of the kingdom of Gwyddno Garanhir. The dyke keeper got drunk one night as a mighty storm blew in, flooding the land and its villages. Ever since, it's been said that the bells of a submerged church can be heard if you stand on the shore at Aberdyfi and listen carefully.

So I listened carefully, very intently. All was quiet except for the swishing of the waves on the seashore. Then I heard it - the sound of the council workman coughing in the carpark, so I set off on the main road back towards Tywyn. Ran at a steady pace for a few minutes then put in some brief bursts of speed before turning back after 18 minutes and repeating the process. When I got back to the prom, I had a breather while pacing out a 30m stretch. Ran this six times flat out walking back each time to rest. Thoroughly invigorated, I walked the short distance back to Awel y Mor for a shower.

Dressed and ravenous, I went up to the dining room where I was greeted by another South Walian. He told me he was from Mountain Ash, had just celebrated his 61st birthday and was in Aberdyfi for the golf. He asked where I was from and where I worked. When I told him I'd retired and was on a cycling trip he said, "I'm retired too. I worked for Mountain Ash council. They offered me a retirement package when I was 50 and I jumped at the chance. My wife still works, so I'm a house husband now - till she retires next year. I'm here with my mate. He made the cut in the golf tournament and I didn't. He should be teeing off just about now".

We compared notes on housekeeping and both agreed wholeheartedly that there's nothing worse than pegging out a line full of washing, then having to bring it back in half an hour later because of rain.

"My wife writes the daily chores on a blackboard for me. The first time I cleaned the toilets I didn't do a very good job. She wrote on the board the following week, 'Toilets today, and make sure you've got your glasses on this time'."

The house husband got his revenge though, "I hoovered the house the next day. It was spotless from top to bottom. Then I put some biscuit crumbs on the hall carpet where she couldn't miss them. When she came home, I had my feet up watching TV. She asked what I'd been doing and I said nothing much. She gave me a ear bashing about the crumbs and then I told her what I'd done. She couldn't help laughing."

Four more golfers came in then. They'd missed the cut as well. Another excellent breakfast which included Jenny the landlady's home made Pembroke sausage. I'm not sure what was in it, but it was like a potato cake. She makes these for veggies because she says they complain about being given baked beans all the time.

Some more golfers arrived as I finished breakfast. Awel Y Mor was full of them, except for me. Inexperienced golfers seemingly, only one of them made the cut. I returned to my room to collect my belongings, then walked back through the dining room to get to my bike. One of the Merthyr couples I'd met the previous night was there and wished me good luck for the rest of my journey.

There's no bridge across the estuary at Aberdyfi. The nearest one is 10 miles away in the town of Machynlleth. A pleasant ride up the valley soon brought me to the old capital of Wales. I turned right across the Dyfi Bridge then took a new cycle path on the wrong side of the road. This ran out 200 yards later at the railway bridge, so it was back to the road again and into the town.

The most prominent thing in Machynlleth is the clock tower. It shows 5 to 10 in the photo I took of it. The clock was a gift from the Marquess of Londonderry to his son Charles, Viscount Castlereagh on his 21st birthday in 1873. Hence its title of the Castlereagh Memorial Clocktower. Some timepiece that! I had a Timex wristwatch for my 21st birthday.

Keeping an eye on my bike, I dismounted to take a look at the tower. It's open underneath, being supported by four pillars. The windows in the tower suggest that it has a stairway running up inside. A walk around the outside revealed no doorway. There was a clue in the shape of a scruffy old aluminum ladder padlocked to one of the pillars. Standing underneath, I looked up to see a padlocked trap door above my head, so that's how they get in.

Machynlleth was recognized as the capital of Wales when Owain Glyndwr assembled a parliament there in 1404. He was also proclaimed King of Wales in the town as well. Owain's wife, Margaret, was incarcerated in the Tower of London in 1408 and from there on his fortunes declined. He was not seen again after 1413 and there is no record of his death nor his place of burial.

*The Mill at Furnace near Machynlleth*

The Parliament House was just a short ride away in Maengwyn Street. I walked under an archway into the rear courtyard, but the building itself was not open. On the other side of the road, were the impressive wrought iron gates of Plas Machynlleth, home of the Londonderry family. I just walked a short distance inside the grounds. The house was not in sight, so I turned back because of an increasingly pressing call of nature.

One pee for 10p. Is that a fair deal? I judged that it was in the circumstances. That's what it cost me to use the Maengwyn Street toilets. They were clean and tidy though.

I cycled slowly out of Machynlleth behind a huge van. Written on the back was, 'International Hauliers - London, Paris, Rome, Madrid and Newtown - but mainly Newtown'.

I enjoyed the next few miles which seemed to be mostly downhill to Furnace. Here I stopped to take a closer look at a water mill at the side of the road. The information sheets around the site told me that a furnace was built here by the Kendall family in 1755. The water mill was used to power two huge bellows to force air through the furnace. When the iron was tapped into sand moulds it was called pig iron because it resembled a feeding sow on her side. It took an acre of local woodland, converted to charcoal, to make one ton of iron. Needless to say, the resources ran out after 50 years when the building was converted to a sawmill. The tapping outlet still had a thin layer of rusting iron on it. The pigs were sent to the Kendall's forges in the Midlands, except for one pig which went to Las Vegas to play the slop machines.

***Electric Railway, Aberystwyth***

Llangynfelin is a tiny village just off the A487. It's thought that Wales' most accomplished poet, Taliesin, was raised there in the 6th century. He was the favourite poet of three different kings during his lifetime. Poets were performers in those days, entertaining the people with the spoken word. It wasn't until the 10th century that his work was recorded in the Book of Taliesin. Blink and you'll miss Tre Taliesin which was named after the poet when he died there. He is buried in the hills above the town in a place known as Bedd Taliesin.

I spotted a bench beside the road in Bow Street where I sat for some light refreshment. I haven't been able to discover why a place in Mid Wales has such an English sounding name. Playtime must have coincided with my break as the sound of laughing, chattering children came to me from the nearby school yard.

Just after Bow Street came a long climb with the reward, on reaching the top, of a grand view of Aberystwyth laid out below me. The steep descent took no time and I was soon looking out to sea from the prom.

On my previous visits to Aber, I never got around to riding the electric train to the summit of Constitution Hill. This time, I chained my bike to the railings outside the ticket office, planning a quick trip up and down. A return was £2.50, but the ticket seller said there was a little problem and there'd be a 10 minute wait. So I boarded the Lord Geraint tram and waited. It was worth waiting. The views from the top were fantastic. Had a quick look at the British Gas beacon (it wasn't lit), then was disappointed to find the camera obscura closed. Caught the Lord Marks tram back.

I was expecting a continuous cable from top to bottom. In fact the two trams are connected by the cable and counterbalance each other. The cable is moved by an electric motor at the top. The two trams pass each other at the half way point going in opposite directions.

Just out of Aberystwyth, a steep climb forced me to walk. Ysgol Llanfarian sticks in my mind because it was outside this school that I got back on the bike again. The road was undulating from here and I was cycling on a nice downhill stretch when I saw written in red on a crumbling wall in front of me the words, 'Cofiwch Dryweryn' - 'Remember Tryweryn'.

In 1965, the Tryweryn Valley, near Bala, was flooded to supply the city of Liverpool with water. It caused great bitterness at the time, especially as the Welsh speaking community of Capel Celyn was forced to move out for the scheme. In 2005, the leader of Liverpool council apologised for the 'insensitivity and hurt' caused by the flooding of Tryweryn.

Roadside benches are a great idea, especially for itinerant cyclists. In Llanrhystud, there was a semi circular grass island at a junction with a side street. In the middle of this lush, little lawn was a large tree with a bench beneath it. I parked my bike against a street sign which said 'Heol Islwyn' and proceeded to unpack my lunch.

A little while later, a long line of children in groups of different ages walked past. There must have been about a hundred in total, heading towards Aberystwyth. Each group was accompanied by two or three adults. Even though no one carried a banner or a money box, I guess it must have been a sponsored walk. Most of them totally ignored me. One or two and several of the adults smiled and said hello. It was such an unexpected sight, I didn't have the presence of mind to ask what they were doing.

Just after the kids passed, a guy walked up from the same direction and sat on the bench next to me. We said hello and as is usual in Wales passed a few comments on the pleasant weather. He was probably about 55, a bit over six foot tall and rather overweight. His green polo shirt didn't quite meet his blue trousers in front.

He took off his navy blue baseball cap and ran his hand over the top of his almost hairless head. "See that?", he said, pointing to his pate with the extra wide parting, "I'm not bald. I'm just a bit taller than my hair, that's all".

He gestured to my bike and asked where I was going. I explained about my journey without seemingly creating much of an impression on him. Then he said, "I had a mate once, dead now mind. Evan his name was, cycled all over the country, he did. Little bloke he was. So small that he was a good inch taller sitting down than when he was standing up. A long time ago, he was looking for this cycling book. He tried the library and the local bookshops around here, but couldn't find it. Mind, it didn't help that he couldn't remember the name of it. All he knew was that it was a book written specially for very short cyclists."

"Evan went to London one day and he was sure he'd get it there. Well, he tried a few big shops without any luck. Then he found a tiny bookshop down a lane. They won't have it here he thought, but went in all the same. Evan told the salesman that he was looking for this book especially for small cyclists. The man said he was in luck, he knew the book and had a copy there. He took the book off the shelf and put it on the counter. Evan said, 'That's it. That's the one. The Titch Biker's Guide to the Galaxy'".

When I arrived at Lima House in Aberaeron, I knocked on the door and rang the bell to no avail. After a brief tour of the harbour and seafront, I returned and to my relief the door was answered straight away. Mr Riley, the landlord, whose first name I've forgotten, is from Yorkshire. He sent me round to the back lane where he was waiting for me at the open garage door. There was everything but a car in the garage. He had to move several boxes of books to make way for my bike.

He then showed me to a large bedroom at the front of the house which had a double bed and ensuite shower room. On the way up the stairs, he explained that his wife, Dawn, owned the Bookworm bookshop in Alban Square. He said that the B+B business was not lucrative, so the bookshop provided a small but welcome boost to their income. Mr Riley was at one time a hospital chef and knows his way around a saucepan. He was unfortunate to suffer a brain haemorrhage some years ago, so he hasn't worked since.

After a shower, cup of tea and a snack, I phoned Euros Lewis. I met Euros for the first time in November 2005 at the launch of my last book. I feel I've known him longer than that though. He featured in the book and we were in touch by e-mail when I was writing it. Euros was the keyboard player in the Welsh language band 'Eliffant' from 1978 to 1984. We arranged to meet in the Harbourmaster Hotel at 6.45pm.

In the meantime, I strolled around the town, buying some sandwiches, cereal bars and fruit from the Spar shop for the next day's trek. I passed the Bookworm bookshop not intending to go in. I had enough in my pannier bags without buying books.

*Aberaeron*

I couldn't resist the temptation. While I was browsing, a lady asked if I needed any help. I guessed it was Dawn Riley from Lima House and I introduced myself. We chatted for a while, then I went back to browsing.

I've been reading Welsh authors lately. I found two books by Emyr Humphreys and one each by Richard Llewellyn and Tristan Hughes which I wanted to buy. Dawn said she operated a postal service and offered to take the books back to Lima House for me so I bought them. My house is getting to look like the National Library of Wales.

Aberaeron was a boat building centre in the 19th century. Many of the houses are named after the ships that were built there, but the Lima was actually built in Aberystwyth. Her captain, John Jones, made wealthy by profitable trips to South America, never fully enjoyed the comforts of his home in Aberaeron. He went down with his ship in the Irish Sea in 1866.

I haven't been there often, but I'm quite fond of Aberaeron. The first time I stayed there was in 1966. I went with my mate Geraint to stay in his Auntie Mat's house. It took nearly a day to get there, on four different buses. Circumstances didn't allow me to go back again for more than 30 years and by then I couldn't remember where Auntie Mat lived. This time, I'd got the address from Geraint in advance and he also told me where his parents had lived. I found and photographed both houses for posterity.

The Harbourmaster Hotel overlooks Aberaeron harbour. I got there early and sat on the wall to wait for Euros. He leads a busy life and was a few minutes late for which he apologised. We went inside and I bought two pints of 'Gwin y Gwan' or as it's commonly known, Guinness. We sat on a bench outside in the warm evening sunshine and I switched on a recorder before asking Euros, "You were born in the Rhondda, what brought you to this area?"

> EL: "Yes, I was born in the Rhondda, but brought up in lots of different areas. I came here to work in Felinfach, which is about six miles up the valley, in an education centre. It works through the medium of theatre and the arts in schools and communities throughout the whole of Dyfed. It's predominantly Ceredigion now. I've left that work now though, I'm freelance now."

> JD: "What exactly does freelance mean?"

> EL: "It means that I'm working on scripts or producing and directing community projects. I'll be working in that context of rural Welsh communities in terms of what's strengthening them and what allows them to integrate people moving in. Losing the main wage earner is another problem. It happened to the mining valleys. Here, it's not happening in one big go. It's something that's chipping away all the time, to the farming communities in particular. Even though it's a minority of people involved in farming, it has a knock on effect to everybody. It's happening to the milk farms in particular, taking the heart out of the community. What I'm trying to do is re-energise that. To lift people's sights back up again."

> JD: "Have you always been a Welsh speaker?"

> EL: "Yes, I have. My mother learned Welsh though."

JD: "Would you call yourself a Welsh nationalist?"

EL: "I don't confine myself in those sort of party terms. I've got no interest in flying the flag, any flag. Our Welsh identity, that's what I'm interested in. That means bringing people together wherever they come from. My grandfather on my Mum's side came from Somerset. My grandmother on the other side was brought up on the Old Kent Road. I think in any family you'll find those sorts of influences. I don't define it in terms of purity of blood. I've no patience with that at all, but in terms of a particular outlook on life and way of dealing with things. In proper communities, people take responsibility for each other. That's the essential thing.

JD: "The old communities always had their doors open."

EL: "I think a lot of that is still there. Particularly in the rural communities. Perhaps not literally with the doors open, but if something happens to somebody, the support they get is tremendous. It overwhelms people who have moved into these areas. They almost can't cope with it, because they're just not used to it. That is the actual thing about the Welsh way of life to me. The language, in a way, demonstrates that. The whole vocabulary is built around doing things together, working together. The Innuits have so many words for snow. We have so many words for working together and places where people work together. That's very important, isn't it?"

JD: "You know Aberaeron well, it's you local town is it?"

EL: "Yes, well partly so. Felinfach, where I work, is halfway between Lampeter and Aberaeron. Lampeter is more of a rural centre for the farmers. Aberaeron is a new town. It was founded 200 years ago next year. It didn't exist before that. There were just a few houses down by the river. It was built, it was created; which means it has a different relationship with the hinterland. There is quite a strong London Welsh influence as well. Lots of families from Ceredigion were so poor that they'd either go to sea or to London to sell milk. That's how my grandmother was brought up on the Old Kent Road. I've done a bit of research into this because I've created a few shows out of it. They worked very hard in London, getting up at 4 o-clock in the morning and working till 10 o-clock in the night, building up a round. Then the train service got better so the milk was actually coming from the countryside. Then out of that business of Welsh dairymen in London came the big dairies, the Express Dairies. Then came the Dairy Trades Confederation and out of that the Milk Marketing Board. So really, the Welsh people from around here have been at the heart of the milk industry. They tended to retire back to this area. Aberaeron in particular, because it was a sort of mini London for them with its Georgian houses and a sort of grace and favour air about it. It was an important place for the people from the valleys too, particularly the Gwendraeth and Amman Valleys. In the miners fortnight, when they closed down, they would descend on places like Llandrindod, Llanwrtyd and Aberaeron."

JD: "What do you think is the best thing about Aberaeron?"

EL: "One of the best things is that the harbour is still an actual harbour and hasn't been developed into a marina. The yachts you see are largely owned by local people. It isn't a sort of jet set fraternity who use it and dump it and you don't see them till next year. Four or five years ago, we did two summers of filming using the harbour as a backdrop for a children's adventure series and we used the local boat people from the yacht club. When I first heard we'd be working with the yacht club, I thought I don't know if I'm going to be able to do this, working with crachach (snobs). But it wasn't crachach at all, it was all local people. You won't find many yacht clubs around Wales that are run by local people. When Reverend Alban Thomas Gwynne built Aberaeron, it became a ship building centre. This side (Harbourmaster) was known as Liverpool and that side was known as Birkenhead. The ship building was on Birkenhead. There were three or four companies building ships here. The last ship launched from here was the Cadwgan in 1883. They would sail to every part of the world, particularly to

South America. They'd be taking wood out and bringing things like guano, which was a fertilizer, back. The sailors were the young people from the farms all around the area. They knew the world much better than we do, I think."

JD: "What's the worst thing about Aberaeron?"

EL: "I think there's always a tension in Aberaeron. Because it's so picturesque it does tend to draw people who think that it's indicative of rural Wales. They think that because it's so beautiful, it doesn't have any problems, which is absolutely wrong of course. It has as many problems as everywhere else. If you say there are serious problems which need addressing here, the political class will say you've got a beautiful place, you're so lucky to be living there. Of course, we are lucky to be living here, but there are still social problems that need to be sorted out. That's part of the problem of living in a beautiful place. People who see it on the surface find it difficult to understand that the beauty is actually masking the problems, the same social problems and tensions that occur elsewhere."

JD: "Do you play in a band now?"

EL: "No, I play the keyboard occasionally with my work. I don't play with a band now."

JD: "Is it only keyboard you play? Do you play guitar?"

EL: "No, not guitar. I can't work guitar out at all. I look at it and it seems obvious because I used to play violin once. It seems to be some version of violin, but it just does my head in. I can play the saw though. I've been learning to play for the last year. One of the things I've developed is a festival of story telling because we don't have professional story tellers in Wales any more. We did have a social class of story tellers - the cyfarwydd. Around the prince's table would be a minstrel, a harpist, a bard and a cyfarwydd. That was the entertainment. We've lost that in terms of professional status, but as an art form it's very alive. When there's a wedding, or even a funeral, very often you'll see a crowd gathering around one person. What's happening? A story's started. Once one story's started, then that will lead on to the next and the next. It's a particular thing with us Welsh. It's something which we have a gift for and I think any community will have this story teller. Over the last two years, we've also been looking for other rural skills or art forms which wouldn't be recognised in a formal way. Playing the saw is one of the things which used to happen when workmen or farm lads got together after work. We found one person, who's 83 years old, from Penuwch, who could play the saw very, very well. Tommy played it so that anybody who was making a noise just quietened down and listened. I thought, well, he's 83, perhaps I should try and find out how he does it. He gave me a few lessons and I've been practising because, like everything else, it's all to do with practise."

JD: "Can you play just any old saw?"

EL: "Oh, and getting the right saw, not all saws will sing. Some of them squeak, some of them don't make a sound at all, but quite a few of them will if you get the bow in the right place and know how to touch it."

JD: "Is getting the right saw a matter of trial and error?"

EL: "Yes, that's what Tommy did. He'd go to the Co-op or the ironmonger and take his bow with him. He'd sit down and try one after another. The Teflon ones aren't particularly good."

At that point, Euros checked his watch. He apologised and said he was late for another appointment. I thanked him for a very entertaining hour with a shake of the hand before he dashed away to his community meeting.

Euros had given me plenty of food for thought, but my thought now turned to food. During my walk through town earlier, I'd discovered a restaurant called Ty Thai - 'West Wales' very first Thai restaurant'. It had a good selection of veggie meals which made it a must for me.

The gaudy red exterior was almost dull compared to the bright pink walls and Chinese dragon tapestry inside. I was greeted warmly by a small, slim, black haired Thai lady. She gave me a menu and invited me to take a seat on the immaculate white wicker furniture in the waiting room.

I ordered a Thai Chang beer which appeared promptly, then settled for a cashew curry from the very varied menu. I flicked through a Wales tourist guide until my meal was ready, which didn't take long.

My drink was carried through to the dining room by a tall, winsome young woman with long black hair and under her tight black t-shirt and trousers you could say she was attractively built. From her accent, I thought she might have been English. After the meal I asked if she lived in Aberaeron.

"No", she said, "I'm from Sussex. I'm studying at Lampeter. I just work here part time to pay my way through college."

I asked what she was studying and she replied, "Anthropology. I've already got my BA. I'm doing an MA now and if that goes well, I'm hoping to do a PhD as well."

Perhaps I should explain here that I only had a vague notion of what anthropology was. I have since turned to the dictionary and this is what it says, 'Anthropology - The study of the natural history of man, including all aspects of his evolution, physical and social'. So now we know.

There were only two other people in the restaurant and the girl from Sussex was so bright and beautiful that I encouraged her to carry on.

"The PhD course involves living in a foreign country and learning to speak their language as well. I haven't definitely decided yet, but I think I would like to go to South America and learn Spanish."

I suggested Patagonia where she could learn Welsh as well. She said she'd picked up a few words of Welsh already, but couldn't speak it. We discussed various aspects of language and Welsh in particular until I started feeling a bit out of my depth and decided it was time to leave.

I've never been waited on by such a charming, beautiful and frighteningly intelligent young lady in my life before and probably never will be again. I made my way back to Lima house at the end of an extremely interesting and enjoyable day. Oh, and the cashew curry was pretty good too.

# *Friday, 16ᵗʰ June*

*There was a young man from Saint David's*
*Bought items on e-bay with brave bids*
*A pair of stuffed finches*
*Some horse saddle cinches*
*And even a collection of rare squids*

On this day in 1829 Apache leader Geronimo was born; in 1890 comedy film star Stan Laurel was born; in 1977 rocket scientist Wernher von Braun died; in 1963 Valentina Tereshkova was the first woman in space.

At 6.15am it was a rather dull and cloudy start to the day. I ran a couple of laps around the playing fields at an easy pace then down onto the north beach. The path petered out so I turned around, went back through the town and along the south beach. Again the path petered out, so I ran around the harbour before going back to Lima House.

Breakfast was in the very pleasant conservatory where the only other guest in the house had started without me. He was a chatty Cockney, probably in his middle 40s. He was slimly built and the hair he had left looked as if it had been carefully groomed flat against his head. His upper body was clothed like a business man with an immaculate blue shirt and matching tie. From the waist down he was definitely on holiday. He wore casual, fawn cotton trousers, plain brown socks and open leather sandals.

We exchanged pleasantries and I asked if he was on holiday, "Yes, I've been here a couple of days now and I'm staying on till July 4th", he said. "I like to combine my spring and summer holidays so that I can have one long break. Are you on holiday?"

I told him about my cycling trip and he said he was a keen cyclist too, "I've got a hybrid bike, which is great for London. It's much quicker than going by car. It's great for learning the 'knowledge' as well. I'm training to be a taxi driver and I can whiz around the routes easy on the bike."

While we were talking, Mr Riley brought me a glass of freshly squeezed orange juice which was delicious. The conversation became a little stilted as we both concentrated on eating. The Cockney ate everything that was put in front of him and I think he would have eaten the plates as well if they'd been edible. He scraped every scrap off every dish of every course. The dishes didn't need washing after he'd finished. My Mam used to say 'waste not want not'. Whether he believed in this old adage or was just trying to get his money's worth is a matter of conjecture. He finished before me and as he left the room he wished me a safe journey.

I thanked Mr and Mrs Riley for their hospitality, said a fond farewell to Aberaeron and was back on the road again by 9 o-clock. There's a long climb out of Aberaeron at the top of which is a village called Henfynyw. It seems to be an insignificant place as you pass through it. It's an important place in Welsh history though, because evidence strongly suggests that St David was brought up and educated there.

A tale is told in New Quay about the smugglers who operated there in the 18th century. More than 100 local people were helping to unload a contraband cargo of salt when some customs officers turned up and tried to arrest them. The locals, naturally, forcefully objected. The officers fired into the crowd, injuring several people. The police were sent for and they arrested the customs officers who had fired their guns. My guess is that those policemen would not have been short of salt for their chips for a few months after that.

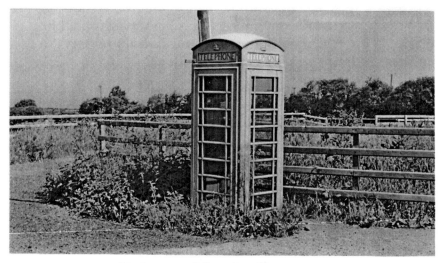

***Endangered Species, Tanygroes***

I had to freewheel with the brakes on all the way down the hill to the new quay which was built in 1835. I walked out along the pier hoping to catch sight of the Bottlenose Dolphins. A resident group of more than 100 live in the sea off New Quay. Right on cue, as I reached the end of the pier, I heard someone say, "There they are, out to the right".

I spent a few magical moments watching the fins pop periodically out of the water as they cruised across the bay no more than 100 yards out to sea, though I now have to divulge that I was deluded. They were not the Bottlenose Dolphins I thought they were. All I saw were short, stubby fins coming out of the water, which means they were probably the harbour porpoises which also populate the sea here.

Dylan Thomas lived in New Quay in1944/5. A strong case has been made for New Quay being the Llareggub of his most famous play 'Under Milk Wood'. Looking from the pier towards the rows of terraced houses rising up the steep hillside I could understand why. Dylan was infamous for his heavy drinking and womanising. He had a wicked sense of humour too, as you'll see if you say Llareggub backwards.

No time to see, the best bits of New Quay. Climbed back up to the A487 which undulated its way south west through the village of Tan y Groes. Here I couldn't believe my luck when I discovered an endangered and increasingly rare species beside the road.

I know you're not going to believe this, so I took a photo for proof. It was a red GPO telephone box! A little faded and neglected mind you, with weeds all around it. The constant encroachment of the mobile phone into our lives will soon render this sad old specimen extinct. It should be removed to the safety of a museum immediately.

*Cardigan*

Llangranog is named after the 6th century saint, Caranog, who is said to have lived for a while in a cave above the beach there. When the Urdd camp was established at Llangranog in 1932, the residents didn't stay in caves - they had the luxury of tents. Many millions of pounds have been spent there since then. The camp now boasts a modern leisure centre and activities like quad biking and dry slope skiing. It's not quite Disney World, but I know a few people who have fond memories of the summer camp at Llangranog.

Talking of Walt Disney, did you know that he was afraid of mice? There's also a rumour rife in America that Disney didn't die, he's just in suspended animation.

It's hard to believe now that in the mid 1800s, Cardigan was one of the busiest international ports in Britain. The silting up of the River Teifi and the advent of the steam ship were mainly responsible for ending this treasure trove of trade. Cardigan now relies largely on a flourishing pleasure boat and tourist industry for its continuing prosperity.

I followed the one way system around the remains of the castle and ended up in the Quay Street car park. Unusually, this is not a Norman castle. The Lord Rhys built the first stone castle on this site around 1170. He was so proud of the finished edifice that in 1176 he invited all the bards, harpists and minstrels from miles around to compete for prizes in a festival. This is widely regarded as the first ever Welsh Eisteddfod.

If you ignored all the vehicles, the Quay street car park was a pleasant enough spot on the riverbank. After a dull start, the sun was shining brilliantly from a bright blue sky, so I found a bench where I could take my mid morning break.

Cardigan is not the home of the woolly jumper, but it is the home of the Cardigan Welsh Corgi. The typical Corgi has fox-like features with a sturdy body set on short legs. The Cardi Corgi also has a long fox-brush tail.

The Queen's Corgis have no tails and live a life of pampered luxury. They sleep in custom made wicker baskets and their diet is specially formulated by the royal vet. At mealtimes, the footman brings in the dog biscuits on a silver salver. A leaked story tells of a bishop, who shall remain nameless, mistakenly taking a dog biscuit from the tray and eating it. To save his embarrassment no one said a thing.

Back on the road, it was all downhill on the B4582 to Nevern. It was a narrow, winding road which meant constant application of the brakes. A fast downhill ride is always exhilarating. At one point, a tractor with four huge wheels almost brought me to a halt. It was a bit of a squeeze to get past.

*Nevern*

I didn't stop at the ancient church of St. Brynach with its famous bleeding yew tree. I went on across the narrow humpbacked bridge over the Afon Nyfer. A stiff climb brought me back up to the A487 and I was soon cycling through Newport. The last time I was in Newport was in 1982. I stayed overnight in the Golden Lion before going on to watch Wales losing 20pts-12 to Ireland in Lansdowne road the next day. It was the end of the Golden Era.

My travelling companions were Byron and Colin who were also my workmates at BP Chemicals in Baglan Bay. Byron was a keen cyclist and even rode to work from his Bynea home on Christmas Day once. He never did it again though because his dinner was spoilt and he got some cold tongue from his wife.

Byron had taken the ferry to Ireland many times. He reckoned the only way to avoid sea sickness was to travel on a full stomach. Immediately on boarding, he devoured a large meal of pie and chips. It was a rough crossing in a force 5 wind. I must admit that I felt queasy, especially after a visit to the toilet where the vomit was slopping back and forth in the urinals. I went out on deck to find Byron leaning on the rail, his face a pale shade of puice and the seagulls enjoying a free feed in the sea below.

*Newport, Pembrokeshire*

A couple of miles inland from Newport is a little place called Cilgwyn. This is the home of author Brian John who has written a five volume novel known as the Angel Mountain Saga. Brian had written many non fiction books before this, but never a novel. The strange thing is that the whole Angel Mountain idea came to him while in a state of fever when he was ill on holiday in the Canary Islands. In the books he depicts Welsh country life in the 18th century in an engaging way through his heroine Martha Morgan, making for a most enjoyable read.

Heading down towards Fishguard, I spotted the harbour and ferry through a gap in the white stone wall on my right. I stopped to take a photo and on the other side of the gate was an empty field with a fabulous view, so I took a lunch break as well.

Fishguard Harbour is not in Fishguard, it's actually a mile away in Goodwick. Officially, Fishguard is the name the harbour has used since its opening in 1906. It's a pity I arrived a couple of months too early to enjoy the centenary celebrations. To make matters worse I'd arrived nine years too late to celebrate the bi-centenary of the last invasion of Britain.

*Fishguard*

In February 1797, a force of 1200 Frenchmen under the Irish American general, William Tate, landed near Carreg Wastad. The French force were dismayed by the local resistance and deceived into thinking that the women in their traditional red shawls and black hats were the British army. The name of Jemima Nicholas will be forever remembered for the part she played in capturing a dozen French soldiers and locking them in St. Mary's church.

When challenged by the local yeomanry led by Lord Cawdor, the French were only too eager to surrender. The Pembroke Yoemanry has the distinction of being the only regiment in the Army to have the name of a British place on its list of battle honours.

Fishguard is also famous for being the setting for the film version of Under Milk Wood starring Richard Burton. Parts of Moby Dick were also filmed there. I've just remembered an interesting film fact, so here's a question for you: which actress wore the same coat in all of her films? Answers on a postcard - no, I'll give you time to think about that one.

The drop down to the River Gwaun was very steep and winding with a one lane road through the Lower Town at the bottom. I had forebodings of a tough climb on the other side. After crossing the little stone bridge, I wasn't disappointed. The hill was so steep I was beaten before I started. I pushed the bike about a quarter of a mile up to the Upper Town.

Back on the bike, I headed out along the A40 thinking I'd surely see a sign soon for such an important city as St. David's. Seeing no sign, I stopped to consult my map. I took the road for Jordanston, after which I got back to the A487, the direct route to our patron saint's city.

When searching for accommodation in St. David's, I came across the Ceffyle Gwynion web site. This B+B is in Croesgoch, six miles east of St. David's. It attracted me greatly though, because the owners stated that it was, 'a totally non-smoking establishment run by vegetarians for vegetarians, where you can relax and enjoy a totally homely atmosphere'.

What a great choice. No disrespect to the other places I stayed in, but Ceffyle was by far the best accommodation on the whole of my journey. I was greeted by landlady, Lynette and her friendly black Labrador. She was short, well built, had short black hair, Lynette that is, not the Labrador and made me feel at home straight away. She assured me that crime was unheard of in Croesgoch, so I left my bike outside while she showed me the room. "There's no one else staying here", she said, "so you can have the en suite at no extra charge. The other room is cheaper, but it hasn't got an en suite.

I was lost in amazement when she let me into the room. It was huge, the twin beds seemed tiny. An archway led through to a separate sitting room with a sea view. In the sitting room were two armchairs, a coffee table, wardrobe, fridge and the accoutrements to make a hot or cold drink. The shower cubicle could have comfortably accommodated three people. All this and breakfast for only £28.

The décor was clean and cream. The carpet had an expensive, deep pile feel to it. The bedding was a matching clean, crisp cream and white. On one of the beds was a white lion, cuddly toy. Quite simply, it was like a hotel executive suite and all mine.

Ceffyle Gwynion is a big, modern bungalow with a huge garage wide enough for three minis. My little bike looked lost in there. As I unpacked, I explained to Lynette that I wanted to visit St. David's, but not by bike. She checked the bus timetable and said if I hurried, I could catch the next bus at 16.36. Moments later, Lynette's husband, Arnold returned home from work. We chatted for a while until I excused myself on the grounds that I had a bus to catch. "Where are you going?" said Arnold. "To St. David's." said I. "If you can wait till about 5 o-clock, I'll give you a lift." said Arnold. "That's very good of you", said I. That gave me a bit longer to shower, dress and have a snack before going down town.

*St. David's Cathedral*

Arnold called for me at five and on the way, he told me, "I'm going to the Cathedral for choir practice. I sing in the choir there." I asked if he was a tenor.

"I sing tenor for St. David's and I also sing bass for another choir." That's a wide range, I was impressed by that. I'm not much of a singer, I can't sing low and I can't sing high.

Arnold told me that they'd lived abroad for a few years, I can't remember where. They bought Ceffyle two years ago. I asked if he could play any instruments, he replied, "No, I can't, my father can. He used to be the cathedral organist. I can read music, though. Good enough to follow the melody of a song anyway." When we arrived at the cathedral, Arnold offered me a lift back after choir practice. I thanked him, but declined because I intended having a meal later. I said I'd get a taxi back.

I may not be a saint, but I do have something in common with St. David, he was a vegetarian. The only liquid he drank was water. That's something we don't have in common. After a look around the ruins of the Bishop's Palace, I visited the ubiquitous gift shop. Not having much room on the bike, I hadn't thought much about souvenirs or gifts. What better place to bring home a gift from than the city of St. David though, but it had to be something small. I bought bookmarkers and locally made chocolate for Ian and his girlfriend Tina and some chocolate for Ad as well.

There was no charge to enter the cathedral. Inside, however, there was a box with a notice inviting a £3 donation which I was happy to comply with. Work began on the cathedral in 1181 on the site of St. David's monastery. Unusually, the roof is made of wood, partly because of poor foundations and also because the building was weakened by an earthquake in 1247. The floor slopes up quite noticeably from the River Alun end to the town end. I was only able to walk around the nave because the choir was closed - for choir practice of course. Arnold and his fellow choristers sounded heavenly.

Lassie - she was the actress who wore the same coat in all of her films. Worth waiting for, wasn't it?!

After a tour of the grounds, I headed for the city centre. I was hoping to find a Spar or similar shop to buy supplies. There were no

Spars in Goat Lane, none in New Street and none in Nun Street. I was on a high when I found a sandwich bar open in High Street.

Cross Square is actually a triangle. I sat on the steps at the base of the cross alongside several other people who had the same idea. A big black and white tom cat crossed the road towards me so I called out to him. He passed within a few feet, cast a look of utter disdain in my direction and walked on. If that had been a dog he would have come to my call. Cats just take a message when you call and they might eventually get back to you.

We have a cat. Her name is Sheba. She's cream with a banded tail and she's 16 years old. After breakfast, I always spread the newspaper out on the table to read it. Sheba will always sit on the paper so I read out to her interesting articles like - 'Ding dong bell, lucky pussy rescued from well', or 'All paws on deck for cat cruiser', or 'Top tips for keeping cats cool'. She seems to enjoy this.

From Monday to Friday I'm home alone except for Sheba. We're good friends. She watches me cooking so I tell her what's for dinner. When she's hungry I ask her whether she wants chicken or tuna. When she returns from a jaunt I ask her where she's been.

One day, she came back with a mouse in her mouth. I managed to take it from her and it was still alive. I said to the mouse, "You poor thing, you must be scared stiff. Don't worry, I'll put you somewhere safe outside." So I did. Then I turned to Sheba and said, "Listen to me. I must be going mad, I've just been talking to a mouse."

It seems possible to judge people's characters by whether they like cats or not. This is not definitive. Amongst some famous cat haters were Genghis Khan, Napoleon and Hitler. The list of famous cat lovers includes Leonardo Da Vinci, Florence Nightingale and Winston Churchill.

One of my pet hates is having to overhear other people's mobile phone conversations. I left the square to sit in the quiet seclusion of the Old Cross Hotel's lush lawn. As I was relating the day's adventures to Ad, a crow landed quite near to me. The poor blighter was bald headed and the other feathers on his body were greying and in poor condition.

He must have been feeling the cold because he toddled unsteadily across the grass and snuggled up to the nearby south facing white washed wall. I've never seen a bird sun bathing before. He seemed to be enjoying the reflected warmth of the wall. He stayed there till I'd finished my phone call. Then, when I got up, he staggered a few steps down the slope, flapped his wings and flew, to my amazement, right over the top of the hotel.

Lynette had recommended the Cartref restaurant on the Square. She said she knew the owner's wife who was also a vegetarian. The Celtic pie was pretty good. It was served with fresh vegetables and the best chips I've ever tasted. They were light, dry, hot and crisp.

There was a young Welsh couple already eating when I arrived. They left soon after. Almost immediately, another young couple came in and sat at the next table to me. It was obvious straight away that they were German. I said hello and asked where they were from. The young man said in excellent English, "We are from Munich. Not the city itself, but a town a few miles away." I said, "Why are you in Wales when the soccer World Cup is on in Germany?" He said, "That is why we are in Wales. It is better not to be there now because it is so crowded." I asked, "Are you staying in St. David's?" The German replied, "No, we are staying in Lampeter. We came to St. David's for a visit today. On Saturday, we are driving to North Wales, to a place called Betws y Coed." his attempt at Betws y Coed made me laugh, but he got pretty close when I told him how to say it.

I asked if they'd been to Wales before. He replied, "No, not to Wales. We have been to Cornwall and Scotland before." The German lad then left the room. His partner had ordered the goat's cheese salad and asked me, "Do you know where the goats are? I have seen in the fields cows and sheep and horses, but no goats." I had to admit that, even though there was a Goat's Lane around the corner, I'd never seen any goats in a field in Wales either.

The young man returned and they reverted to their native language while they ate. I enjoyed a Mississippi Mud Pie smothered with cream, another pint of lager and then asked the waiter to direct me to the taxi rank.

The taxi driver was very sociable and talked a lot. He had plenty to say about the council and the government. He also reckoned that the way to solve traffic congestion was to only allow cars that had been paid for in full to use the roads. Isn't it strange that the only people who know how to run the country are too busy cutting hair or driving taxis.

He enlightened me to the tune of £13 which I made up to £15 as befits the occupant of an executive suite of rooms.

# *Saturday, 17<sup>th</sup> June*

*There was anold lady from Tenby*
*Who went on a day trip to Denbeigh*
*She fell in the fountain*
*Then rolled down the mountain*
*And even got stung by a hen bee*

On this day in 1025 the first king of Poland Boleslaw the Brave died; in 1945 Belgian cyclist Eddy Merckx was born and the current mayor of London, Ken Livingstone, was born; in 1946 Barry Manilow was born.

Up at 6.15am. The sun was already shining. Ran at a steady pace down to Porthgain on the coast. Took a few photos and ran back up a lot slower than I ran down.

Porthgain was a busy port for about 100 years until the last cargo left for Liverpool in 1934. It must have been a port for much longer than that as the Sloop Inn dates back to 1743. One of the early cargos exported was slate from the quarries of North Pembrokeshire which is of inferior quality to that of North Wales. Porthgain later became more famous for its crushed granite and bricks.

With high headlands on either side of the harbour entrance, it was necessary to position beacons on the hilltops as an aid to navigation.

The brickworks have long since disappeared. The crushed granite hoppers can still be seen on the quay side. The villagers now rely largely on fishing and tourism for their livelihood.

*Porthgain*

All that water in the harbour and the Irish Sea beyond made me think what a strange and wonderful world we live in. Hydrogen is an explosive gas. A fire can't burn without oxygen. When these two elements are combined they become water, which is used to put out fires.

Arnold was just leaving for work when I walked into the kitchen for breakfast. He planted a proper kiss on Lynette's lips before leaving, in such a natural show of affection, it caused me no embarrassment at all.

While I ate my Weetabix, Lynette was cooking my vegetarian sausages. She is a warm and sociable person who is easy to talk to. She told me that she'd been married to Arnold for eight years and continued by saying, "He was already a vegetarian when I met him. Before we married, he suggested I give it a try. It wasn't a condition of our marriage or anything, but I wanted Arnold so I became a veggie as well.

At that time we were living in Hampshire and just after we married I had a brain haemorrhage. I was lucky to survive. They did a brain scan on me and I watched it on the monitor. It was fascinating. I gave them permission to film my operation and they're using the DVD to train new brain surgeons now. I'd love to see it one day.

We're both from this area originally, so because of my problem we decided to move back. Ceffyle was the first place we looked at. We loved it so much we bought it there and then.

When I was a young girl, I lived on a farm planting and picking potatoes. The haemorrhage has left me with a weak right arm. I have a job to pick up one potato now, let alone a sackful like I used to then.

Last year, I came out of the upstairs bathroom with nothing on and fell down the stairs. I broke my arm and just couldn't get up. Luckily Arnold was home. He came out to the hall where I was lying, but he couldn't move me either. He wanted to phone for an ambulance, but I wouldn't let him till he got some clothes for me. He reckoned that they'd probably seen worse sights in their job than a nude woman with a broken arm. The worst thing about it was I broke my left arm, my good one, which made life really awkward for a while. The arm is fine now though."

She asked where I'd eaten the night before. I told her about Cartref and the German couple. She said that when I was out a German couple called there looking for a B+B. They also said that they were in Wales because the World Cup was on in Germany. They didn't stay because the German lady insisted on having an en suite room. I felt guilty then because I had the en suite and I hadn't booked it. Lynette told me not to worry; it had been her decision to put me in there.

I could have listened to her all day, but time was passing and I had to be on my way. I set out on the B4330 for Haverfordwest, bypassing St. David's as I'd already spent a fair bit of the previous day there. I saw only two road signs early on so at every junction I avoided crossing any white road lines. I guessed I'd probably gone wrong when I passed RAF Brawdy which was not on my route.

The RAF left Brawdy in 1992. It's currently occupied by the Royal Corps of Signals under the name of Cawdor Barracks. I kept going until I finally came to a junction with the A487. Here, I turned to the left for Haverfordwest.

Soon after, the road twisted down steeply to Newgale. It ran flat for about half a mile and, yes you've guessed it, climbed so steeply away from the coast that I had to get off and push. I did get a good photo of Newgale Beach on the way up though. It's a pity I didn't have my board with me, otherwise I'd have stopped to try out Newgale's two mile stretch of surf.

Haverfordwest has the distinction of being granted both a town and county charter. Its central Pembrokeshire position on the Western Cleddau contributed to its early importance and still does today, although to a lesser extent. Christian Bale, star of the 'Batman Begins' film, was born in Haverfordwest in 1974. Gruff Rhys, singer with the Super Furry Animals band, was born there in 1970 as was Welsh soccer star, Simon Davies in 1979.

I cycled over the Cleddau twice as I passed through Haverfordwest. On the southern edge of the town, I spotted a bus shelter with seats in it. Here I stopped for my mid morning break.

I'd only just opened my flask when I noticed a flashy, open top BMW heading out of town. It was being driven by a young man sporting an equally flashy pair of gold rimmed sunglasses. Two minutes later, he came by heading back in to town. Then, as I was about to leave, he came by again heading out of town. He seemed to be a bit of a poseur and I reckon he was only wearing dark glasses so that he could ogle the girls without being caught at it.

Just after Neyland, there was a great view from the road bridge of the marina below. I parked my bike carefully against the railings and crossed the road to take a photo. When I turned back, the bike had fallen on its side, spilling the contents of my bar bag onto the road. In a panic, I ran back to pick everything up and, luckily, there was no damage done. I can only assume that the slip stream from a large vehicle had pulled the bike over. It wasn't windy and I didn't see it happen.

Brunel is regarded as the founder of Neyland. He decided to make the little village the terminus of his South Wales Railway in 1856. The town enjoyed 50 years of expansion and prosperity as the ferry port for Ireland until Fishguard took over in 1906.

Gordon Parry was born near Narberth in 1925 and educated in the schools of Neyland. He was a lifelong member of the Labour Party who never became an MP even though he stood in four elections. He was a skilled public speaker, but better known for his role as chairman of the Wales Tourist Board. He was created Baron Parry of Neyland in 1975. His love for Pembrokeshire was such that he lived in the county till he died in 2004. At the height of his fame his ready humour was highlighted when Who's Who quoted one of his pastimes as being 'watching the Welsh rugby team win the Grand Slam'. Oh for those golden, glory days once more.

A short ride brought me to the Cleddau Bridge. This was completed in 1975, but not before part of it collapsed and nearly destroyed the houses below. It's a toll bridge, £1.50 for buses and lorries, 75p for cars and vans, 35p for horses, horse drawn vehicles and motorbikes. Pretty cheap compared to both the Severn Bridges. Even better for me, cycles were free. The bridge has a cycle path and half way across I stopped to take a photo of the view upriver. This time I didn't even get off my bike. I just straddled it while taking the snap.

Pembroke Dock became a Naval shipyard in 1814 toward the end of the Napoleonic War. During her reign, Queen Victoria chose the shipwrights of Pembroke to build three royal yachts. They were named Victoria and Albert I, II and III.

The docks played an important part in the production of ships for the WWI effort only to be closed down in the depression of 1926. The RAF became established in Pembroke Dock in1930. During WWII, Sunderland and Catalina flying boats were based there. The RAF left in 1959 after which PD benefited from the development of the oil industry in Milford Haven and the Irish Ferries service to Rosslare.

There's one question that can be asked all day, you'll get a different answer to that question, yet every answer is correct. What is that question? It was only a short distance to Pembroke town where I dismounted on the river bridge. I got a good shot of the castle from the observation platform when a youngster, no more than nine or ten years old asked me, "What's the time mister?" - That's the question, the answer is always different yet always correct. As long as your watch is right.

***Pembroke Castle***

William Marshall, Earl of Pembroke, began transforming the wooden fort at Pembroke into a stone structure in 1189. Henry Tudor was born in the castle in January 1457 and was crowned Henry VII in 1485. Henry never returned to Pembroke after his coronation. This was my second visit to Pembroke, I wonder if I'll ever go back again.

Part of the Pembrokeshire National Park is given over to Army training. Castlemartin belonged to the Cawdor Estate until it was requisitioned by the government in 1938. The training area covers almost 6000 acres, much of which is still farmed. Access to the Coast Path is allowed when the guns are not being fired. My little bike has no armour plating, so needless to say, I stayed clear of Castlemartin.

Although the bishops of St. David's had a nice little pad near the cathedral, they were a worldly lot and liked to retreat from religion at

Lamphey. The ruins of the Bishop's Palace at Lamphey are largely the work of Henry de Gower who also built the palace at St. David's in the 14th century.

Another castle now and the journey's not over yet. Built by William de Barri in the 12th century, Manorbier is more like a fortified manor house. Most Norman castles have a keep isolated from the outer walls, whereas the keep at Manorbier is incorporated into the wall.

Manorbier is worth a mention because it was the birthplace of Giraldus Cambrensis (Gerald of Wales) in 1146. He was the son of William de Barri and the Welsh princess Angharad. He was an intelligent and well travelled man who wrote many books, 17 of which still survive today.

***Tenby***

I found an interesting website on Manorbier castle. I assume it was written by    a person who was not born in Britain. It says, 'Giraldus, one of the most important figures of the Welsh medieval history, had his Christmas at Manorbier in the 12th century.'

The area is described thus: 'The impact with the village of Manorbier will be strange to you positively. In fact, the castle and all the surrounding zone are carefullied lay down in one tightened valley cut from two torrents that flow beyond the beaches in the bay of Manorbier, rendering the entirety much scenographic'.

After Lydstep, it was only a short step to Tenby. I had to stop once for a photo shoot when I spotted a cracking view of Caldey Island through a hole in the hedge.

Caldey's Welsh name is Ynys Byr after the 6th century abbot Pyro. The present monks belong to the Cistercian order. They keep a silence, study, do manual work and pray. In fact they pray seven times a day, the first being Vigil at 3.30am, The monks of Caldey are early to bed and early to rise, which, as my Mam used to say, should make them healthy, wealthy and wise.

The monks realized some time ago that it takes money to maintain even their modest lifestyle. To this end, they have developed a range of home made products which has made the monastery self sufficient. The Caldey Collection includes books, biscuits, chocolate, perfume and first day stamp covers.

'By' is the Viking word for barn. Does that mean there are ten barns in Tenby? I wasn't staying in a barn, I'd booked a room in the Hammonds Park Hotel. After consulting the map, I rode through the town to where I thought the hotel should be. There was no street sign to be seen anywhere. I stopped to ask a young man carrying a little girl on his shoulders if he knew where Narberth Road was. "This is it. You're in it" he said. "Do you know where the Hammonds Park Hotel is?" I said. "Right in front of you. I can see the sign just up the road there", he said. I only had 50 yards to go and was soon cycling into the forecourt of the hotel.

I rang the bell at reception and waited ages for a reply. A young man dressed in long, khaki shorts and a black t-shirt eventually emerged from a secret inner sanctum below the stairs. I gave him my name, he checked a book, then asked me to wait while he found out which room I was in.

My Mam used to say, 'Hir yw bob aros' (Long is every wait). It seemed like ages, but was probably no more than a couple of minutes before he came back and gave me the key to room number nine.

John Lennon's magic number was nine. He was born on the 9th October, 1940. The first address he lived at was 9 Newcastle Road. His second son, Sean, was born on his 35th birthday 9th October, 1975. Lennon died on 8th December, 1980 in New York which was the 9th in Britain. He wrote two songs with nine in the title - 'Revolution 9' and '#9 Dream'. Some time after his death I wrote a song in tribute to John called 'No. 9 Song' subtitled 'Lord Have Mersey On Us'. The lyrics went something like this :-

*I don't want to be a soldier* and I don't believe at all

That *happiness is a warm gun* now my back's against the wall

*Power to the people, come together* they all say

Is *revolution* the answer, we'll find out on judgement day

 

*A day in the life* of a *nowhere man* living on *borrowed time*

He's *crippled inside* and needs some *help* and his life's not worth a dime

*Watching the wheels go round* and round, he's a very *jealous guy*

*Whatever gets you through the night* is the maxim he lives by

 

*How do you sleep* in the middle of the night, can you cope with your *no.9 dream*

Was it *Lucy in the sky with diamonds* or was it *strawberry fields* with cream

*Give me some truth* cos your *mother* should know that you're a *beautiful boy*

It's *just like starting over* and this *woman* gives you such joy

 

Even though you've gone away, far *across the universe*

You'll still be with us here in your every song and verse

*Working class* you were I know, but a *hero* all the same

How could you *imagine* that this life would lead to so much fame

*Happy Christmas, war is over*

*Let's give peace a chance*

*Nobody told me* these *mind games*

Would put me in a trance


All the words in italics are titles of songs that John Lennon wrote.

Before I went up to room nine, the receptionist was good enough to show me where to park my bike. The hotel is built on a slope. At the back is a high retaining wall with a narrow alleyway leading into the kitchen. This was where I left my bike safely out of sight.

It was a big room with a double bed that creaked like Methuselah's 900 year old joints. The en suite had a shower over the bath. Everything was clean and tidy, if a little old fashioned, especially after such superb quarters in Croesgoch.

Tenby was the birthplace of the actor Kenneth Griffith on 12th October, 1921. Only a week after my visit, I was saddened to hear of his death on the 25th of June at the age of 84. He appeared in more than 80 films and was equally at home in front of the television cameras. He was regarded as a world expert on the Boer War about which he made a series of documentaries. Griffith was an outspoken character and some of his documentaries were so controversial that they were banned. He was highly regarded as an actor and film maker and Tenby can be justifiably proud of this talented and passionate man.

After a shower and a reviving cup of tea, I phoned Geraint in Carmarthen to give him a progress report and to tell him I was on schedule for my stopover the next day.

Sunshine on my shoulders makes me happy. I was really happy as I set off to walk to the town centre. Only a few minutes down the road I spotted an old iron milestone set into the wall. I'm as curious as a cat, so I stopped to have a look at it. Written on the wrought iron was '10 miles 970 yards to Narberth'. There was no date, but at the bottom was 'Marychurch Founders'. Now that's what I call accuracy in an age when sat nav didn't exist.

$2+2 = 4$. If it wasn't for Robert Recorde, born in Tenby in 1557, we would still be writing 'is equal to'. Recorde trained to be a doctor of medicine at Cambridge University. He was physician to King Edward VI as well as controller of the Royal Mint. He also taught mathematics and wrote several books on the subject. It was in his 'Whetstone of Wit' in 1857 that he introduced the equals sign that we still use today. The following year, he was sued for defamation and arrested for debt. He died in Southwark prison in1558. Recorde also invented the word 'zenzizenzizenzic' to denote the $8^{th}$ power of a number. It has more zs in it than any other word in the English language. For some reason, it didn't quite catch on.

There's a splendid new lifeboat station in Tenby. It was built to accommodate a new computer controlled Tamar class lifeboat. The boat is called 'Haydn Miller' in honour of the person whose bequeathed donation paid for it. Visitors can view the boat, see a film and browse in the gift shop. The crew have their own separate access so visitors can even watch a launch.

I bought a bookmark in the shop which I'm actually using now in the notebook that I'm writing this journal in. There was a white haired old gentleman on the till. I asked if any of the crew were in the station at the moment. "No", he replied. "They're all on call. The station is unmanned except for a fitter. Even he's not here now, though. He finished work at lunchtime".

I asked him if there'd been a shout lately. "Well, about three weeks ago, I was talking to a customer who said he'd love to see the boat being launched. He went out of the shop and was on the viewing platform when the alarm sounded. He saw all the crew coming in and launching the lifeboat. He filmed it all and went away absolutely delighted."

That guy was lucky to get his action film, but we mustn't forget that his good fortune was because of someone else's misfortune. After all, the lifeboat's role is to rescue people in danger of losing their lives. They do a fantastic job and it's all voluntary.

Augustus Edwin John was born in Tenby on 4th January, 1878. He was a very popular painter who became famous for his portraits. They were sometimes too lifelike as in the case of Lord Leverhulme who cut out the head on his portrait because he didn't want anyone to see it. John was also something of a ladies man. His two marriages and frequent flirtations begetting eight children that he knew of. His sister, Gwen, though not so famous, was also a very talented artist. Augustus died in October, 1961.

Walking up through High Street, I noticed an accountant's office. Handling other people's money as a way of make a living would never appeal to me somehow. I don't know any poor accountants though. It's been said that old accountants never die, they just lose their balance.

At the top of High Street is a nice fruit and veg shop. The sign above the pine end window says, 'Floral Corner, C. H. Handicott and Sons, Est.1939'. I went inside and asked for some bananas. The counterhand, a man in his late 50s, (could it have been Mr. Handicott?) asked, "Do you want green bananas or yellow ones for eating now?" I bought some yellow ones as well as some red apples which he recommended. The personal service was great and I would definitely go there again.

Across the road, I topped up my phone card in W. H. Smith and after buying some sandwiches in Londis the other side of town, I succumbed to temptation. Passing back through the town wall, I stopped to look at the display of cream cakes in the window of Fecci's Ice Cream Parlour. The sight of those cakes and the smell of coffee percolating out through the open door was too much. Long distance cycling makes you hungry. It didn't take me long to scoff a cream and jam scone washed down with a huge cup of hot coffee.

I took my purchases back to the hotel where I phoned home. Earlier in the day I'd spotted a nice looking restaurant in Tudor Square called the Baytree. They had a good vegetarian choice, so that was where I headed for my evening meal. It was only 7.15pm when I got there and it was already busy. I asked for a table and was told initially that I'd have to wait at least half an hour. The waitress came back in only a couple of minutes and said a table had just become available. She explained that they only allowed a certain number of tables to be booked in advance so that people like myself wouldn't be disappointed.

When I sat down there were only a couple of empty tables. These were occupied by the time my meal arrived. I thoroughly enjoyed the broccoli and stilton crepes with roasted onions, courgettes and aubergines. The chips were nice, but couldn't match the previous night's in Cartref.

There was a constant buzz of conversation. Everyone seemed to be enjoying themselves. I couldn't make out what was being said, even on the adjacent tables. It was still warm outside, the meal made me even hotter till I could feel the sweat trickle down my legs and back. As soon as I'd finished eating, I paid the bill and left.

I walked down to the Castle Beach where I sat on the rocks watching some fishermen while the sun settled into the west and the tide trickled in. They didn't catch anything, but the antics of a young boy with his own small rod kept me amused. He hadn't quite mastered the art of casting. Every time he tried, the bait landed a few yards in front of him or went sideways over the lines of the adults alongside him. Eventually they told him to try further along the beach. He moved 20 or 30 yards away where he still continued to make a mess of his casting. He got fed up after a few minutes and went back to tantalise the adults again, until one of them made a good cast for him. Then he abandoned the rod and went to play in the rock pools near me. I was about to leave when a small, mongrel puppy came jogging up to me. I called him and he came right up to me frantically wagging his tail, jumping up and licking my hands. His owner soon appeared, called the dog to order and said hello to me. He was probably about my age, 57 or thereabouts. He wore a beige t-shirt, blue jeans and off white, suede slip-on shoes. His hair, white and thinning, was combed back in what we used to call a slash-back style. He was average height, a bit overweight and his cheeks were so red that it looked as if he'd just run 10Km. He also had two thickish gold chains around his neck, worn outside his t-shirt.

He mentioned the good weather then asked if I was on holiday. I told him about my cycle journey and then he said, "You like sport do you? I don't. I don't know anything about it. I've never been to a soccer or rugby match. Do you know Alan Curtis? He used to play soccer for Swansea and Leeds and Wales. He's a coach with Swansea now. I saw him on TV last week.

Mind, I don't watch TV much, hardly at all really. I can't stand those soaps. I don't watch Eastenders. That Pat, she gets on my nerves. She's always quarrelling with everybody.

Are you married? I got married for the second time 10 years ago. This one's not the same as the first one. Won't go anywhere. I haven't been out for ages. We went to Aberystwyth last week. Only to see her sister though.

I like the theatre myself. My grandfather used to be a music hall performer. He had an animal act. Trained dogs and birds to do tricks. He was marvellous, so I'm told. My Dad used to tell this story about my Grandpa's show. A dancing duck. That was the finale of his act. It always brought the house down. The music played, my Grandpa put the duck on a tin drum. He'd do this dance and the curtain would go down. The audience went mad. Never failed. Except for one night. He put the duck on the tin drum and nothing happened. They booed him off the stage."

He remained silent for a moment, so I asked, "What went wrong?", to which he replied, "The candle went out".

And so to bed.

# Sunday, 18th June

*There was a young man from Carmarthen*
*Who's bike was an old penny farthen*
*When decimals came in*
*He was angry as sin*
*And decided to buy a new car then*

On this day in 1812 the USA declared war on Great Britain; in 1815 the Duke of Wellington defeated Napoleon; in 1942 Paul McCartney was born; in 1983 Sally Ride was the first American woman in space.

Woke at 6.20am. After the ablutions and warm up, I ran down through the town until I came to a level section of road alongside a small park. I stopped to admire the view from the park which is on a hill overlooking the golf course and coast. I paced out 100m here and ran that distance five times flat out, walking back to recover. Also ran 5x30m flat out as well.

Halfway through this session, an old gent strode purposefully past. He must have been 75 with white, well groomed hair and moustache. He was smartly dressed in white shirt and dark tie, grey trousers with knife sharp creases and a black blazer with a badge on the breast pocket. He had a military bearing and gave me a snappy, "Good morning", as he went by. I hope I'm as fit as he looked when I'm that age.

As I finished the session, some people walked past on the other side of the road. The man and woman, who were probably in their 30s, said nothing. Their son (I assumed) stopped and said, "Hey mister, how far have you run?" "About a couple of miles", I said. He was about 10 years old, had longish, black curly hair, chubby cheeks and was a fair bit overweight. "Do you like running?" he asked. "Yes, I do", I said, "I love it. Do you?" "No, I don't like it", he said, "it's boring. Besides you've run out of breath now". "No, it's alright", I said, "I haven't run out, I've still got some left". With that his mother called. He gave me a cheeky grin, poked out his tongue and waddled away. I couldn't help laughing as I ran back to the hotel.

On my way up Narberth Road, I noticed a sign on my right. It said, 'Mayfield Drive leading to Slippery Back'. Thank goodness I didn't have to run up there. It was hard enough going up without slipping back.

After a shower, shave, shampoo and lav visit, I was more than ready for breakfast. Fruit juice, cereal, vegetarian cooked breakfast with quorn sausages and plenty of toast washed down with a pot of tea. With the packing finished, I was ready to leave. Almost ready, except that I had a funny feeling in the pit of my stomach. Another visit to the toilet was called for. A certain looseness, but, I hoped, nothing serious.

On the A487, I turned right at the first roundabout to drop down a steep hill into Saundersfoot. Many, many years ago, a Walter Elisaunder lived in this region. It seems likely that Elisaunder's Ford may have given rise to Saundersfoot's present name. During the 19th century, Saundersfoot was busy exporting local anthracite coal. when the coal industry collapsed, it became a popular seaside resort where tourists can indulge in fishing, walking and all types of water sports.

The centre was already crowded by 10.00am. There was a traffic jam through which I had to wend my way before tackling a tough climb out of town. This set the pattern for the day as a series of downs and ups through each village followed.

The next port of call was Wiseman's Bridge which owes its name to Andrew Wiseman, a 14th century land owner. The village had some famous visitors in August 1943. Winston Churchill, Admiral Mountbatten and General Eisenhower were present to watch rehearsals for the D-Day landings.

***Amroth***

For Tolkien fans, this little digression could be interesting. If you're not a fan, then you could be bored. Amroth is a name that appears in 'The Lord of the Rings' as well as on the map of Wales. Lord Amroth doesn't play a major part in the book, he's more of an historical character. Tolkien says, 'Of old he was an Elven King, A lord of tree and Glen', and there's not much more. There is also a city called Dol Amroth in Middle Earth. A significant character called Imrahil was prince of this place.

The interesting thing is that Tolkien, a professor of philology, was fascinated by the Welsh language. He based his own invented Elven tongue on the sounds of Welsh words.

In his younger days, Tolkien lived near a railway line in Birmingham where he watched coal trucks go by with names like Senghenydd, Penrhiwceiber and Nantyglo written on them. I don't know whether he just took the name Amroth directly from the village name or thought he'd invented it. I just find his books fascinating. I've read TLOTR 13 times. I'm overdue to read it again now. I've got to finish writing this book first though. I've summarised TLOTR in my favourite rhyme form, a limerick:-

*A hobbit who lived in the Shire*

*Had all that his heart could desire*

*Then a wizard one day*

*Came and sent him away*

*And said, 'Throw this ring in the fire'*

To continue. Amroth beach is an archaeologists dream. When the tide is out the remains of a fossilised forest become exposed. Animal fossils and Neolithic flints have also been found there.

Amroth is the easternmost starting point of the Pembrokeshire Coast Path. I didn't discover this till I got home. So much for my research. The path runs to Wiseman's Bridge and then through three tunnels to Saundersfoot. The tunnels were excavated to allow coal trains to travel to the port at Saundersfoot. I could have saved myself a couple of downs and ups by using this path.

Pendine Beach boasts seven miles of firm, flat sand. Early pioneers of speed Malcolm Campbell and John Godfrey Parry-Thomas set five world land speed records there between 1924 and 1927. Parry-Thomas was killed in March 1927 when his 27 litre car, 'Babs', crashed. Locals buried his car in a sand dune where it remained until 1969 when it was recovered and restored. It's now on permanent display in the Pendine Museum of Speed. No speed records for me as I plodded painfully up the long slope out of Pendine

On the outskirts of Llanmiloe, I passed a parked Land Rover. With my eagle eye, I spotted a sticker in the back windscreen which said, 'If you can see this where the hell is my caravan'.

***Laugharne Castle***

A little further on I stopped for a snack. There was a farm across the road and, as I sat down, a black and white sheep dog came out. He looked as if he was limping, then I realized he only had three legs. One of his hind legs was missing. The poor chap seemed quite happy. He was friendly, didn't bark at me, then sat down and gave me the old, sad-eyed stare.

I threw him a biscuit which he gobbled up in no time, and then he sat there looking at me a doleful expression on his face. I could only stand it for a couple of minutes. A sad eyed doggy was no aid to my digestion. I bundled my biscuits back into the bar bag and cycled off. I finished my snack sitting on a grassy bank half a mile further on.

In the field behind me was a group of farm workers with a tractor and trailer. They were a mixture of young and old and they chatted and laughed as they worked. It was a rare country scene because farming has been on the decline in Wales for many years now. Heavy industry has declined as well. The Port Talbot Steel Works employed over 20,000 people at its peak. I think it's down to about 3,000 now.

In fact, I read in the paper a few weeks ago that more people are employed by Indian restaurants in Britain than in steel, shipping and coal combined now. It also said that we export Chicken Tikka Masala to India and they export computer software to us.

Dylan Thomas loved Laugharne. He said in his last BBC broadcast that 'there is nowhere like it anywhere at all'. One of the most photographed and painted places in the village is the Boathouse where Dylan lived with his family for the last four years of his life. Above the Boathouse is the garage which Dylan used as his workroom. Here, in between his letter writing, reading and perhaps a beer induced doze, he wrote some of his best poems. Most of 'Under Milk Wood' was also written there.

The stonework structure of Laugharne Castle was largely the work of the De Brian family in the late 13th century. The history of the castle is complicated. It was occupied by Normans, Welsh, Royalists and Roundheads over the years.

One of the reasons for Dylan moving to Laugharne was his friendship with Richard Hughes who lived in Castle House. Hughes is a somewhat neglected writer. His most famous novel, published in1929, is 'A High Wind in Jamaica' which was also made into a film. He also wrote the first ever radio play called 'Danger'. It was broadcast by the BBC in 1924. I've read all of Richard Hughes' novels and enjoyed them immensely.

Dylan's mother, Florence, lived in the Boathouse until her death in 1958. The boathouse is now a heritage centre preserved as it would have been in Dylan's days. There is a rumour that the ghost of Florence haunts the house. Strange goings on like books on the floor, pictures that have moved and lights being switched on have been reported by the staff.

Talking about death, our local undertaker has just put up the cost of burial. He's blamed it on the cost of living. And have you noticed that everybody has their favourite song played at their funeral these days. I can't decide whether to have 'Return to Sender' or, because I'm going to be cremated, 'Smoke Gets In Your Eyes'. I once heard of a butcher whose funeral hymn was 'And the Sheep Shall Safely Graze'.

Last winter, I went for a run around the Corus reservoir near the Margam Crematorium. It was very cold, but the sun was shining from a bright blue, cloudless sky and there was no wind at all. The lake lies alongside the M4 on its eastern shore and the Swansea-London railway on the other side. As I ran through the trees on the motorway side, I noticed smoke all around me and I couldn't avoid breathing it in. There must be a fire somewhere, I thought. Halfway along the other side of the lake, I looked across to see a huge cloud of blue smoke hanging motionless over the trees I'd just run through. In the middle of the smoke cloud was Margam Crematorium.

After passing through St Clear's, I joined the A40 dual carriageway. At the top of a long rise, I needed to turn right to take the road for Llansteffan. With no roundabout, this meant crossing over four traffic-laden lanes. I pulled over on to the left hand verge and had to wait two or three minutes until a gap appeared between the hurrying horseless carriages. I made it safely to the central reservation then had to repeat the process to complete the crossing.

***Holy Trinity Church, Llanybri***

The sign said six miles to Llansteffan. If the road had been flat it would have been only three miles probably. I had to get off and push four or five times. At the top of the first hill the road passed through a farm called 'Hendre' where three sheep dogs rushed out of a barn to bark at me. Luckily there was a wire mesh fencing them in. The road passed through a second farm called Coombe Hill. Before I could work out why Coombe Hill was at the bottom of the valley, a veritable pack of dogs was barking away belligerently. They were also behind a fence, all except one that is. He chased me for 30 yards then gave up as I left his territory.

Llanybri is a small farming community with a history going back to the Stone Age. I entered the village like I imagine the Stone Age citizens would have done - on foot, although I don't think they would have been pushing a pack laden bike.

Some writers achieve fame and fortune in their own lifetime. Others, perhaps of equal ability, never trouble the taxman. One such under-appreciated poet was Lynette Roberts (1909 - 1995). She was born in Buenos Aires of Welsh ancestry and lived in Llanybri from 1939 to 1949. Dylan Thomas was best man at her marriage to Keidrych Rhys. 'Poem From Llanybri' is one of her better known works and she is buried in the Holy Trinity churchyard at Llanybri.

I took a photo of the church. It's unusual in that it used to have a spire which, for some unknown reason, is now a sawn-off octagonal tower. Quite by accident, I spotted a small, black headstone which said, 'Lynette Roberts. Poet, 1909-1995'. It might sound morbid, but I took a photo of that as well.

It was all downhill from Llanybri to Llansteffan. When I reached the seafront, there was a strong wind of almost sandstorm proportions blowing across the car park. I took shelter on a bench beside the tea cabin to snack on some sandwiches, nuts, banana and tea. For some reason I felt guilty about drinking my own tea while sitting next to a business that was trying to make a living selling it.

Some sand blew around the cabin onto my sandwiches which made them crunchy. My mind went back to those sunny seaside days on Aberafan Beach when sand covered sandwiches were the snack of the day.

A little interlude here. I've just returned from watching the evening news on TV. One of the items concerned a tornado that hit Bow Street overnight. If you remember, earlier in the book I described sitting on a bench in Bow Street in wonderful weather listening to the kids playing happily in the school behind me. It was a totally different picture on the news. Fences and trees were flattened. Roofs and chimneys were ripped off and a mobile office was blown clear across the railway line. Luckily no one was hurt.

Tornado would be a good name for a group of politicians, I think. A tornado of MPs. Why? Because a tornado is a spinning mass of hot air.

Quite a few people passed through the car park, leaning into the wind like walking lampposts with clothes on. My view of the Tywi Estuary was restricted from where I was sitting. That's why Llansteffan Castle was built on a nearby hilltop. Fortifications going back to the Iron Age have been found there. As ever, the remains of the current stone walled castle date to the Norman period. A major part of the work was undertaken by the De Camville family.

Only eight miles to Carmarthen, only 24 hours to Port Talbot. With the wind behind me all the way it took no time to reach Tanerdy. There's a very steep climb up to Geraint's house and I made no attempt to ride up it. I walked the last quarter of a mile.

Geraint has lived in Carmarthen since 1976. It's a town with a huge history dating back to the Demetae people of the Iron Age. Known as Moridunum when the Romans colonised it in 75AD, Carmarthen is probably the oldest town in Wales. The Normans took over 1000 years later. The remains of the castle, built by William Fitz Baldwin, can be found behind the council offices.

The wizard, Merlin, is rumoured to have been born in a cave near Carmarthen. It was said that if Merlin's Oak in Priory Street fell then the town would also fall. When it died, the remains of the rotten tree were removed to the museum. I can vouch for the fact that

Carmarthen town still stands, except for the bits they're knocking down for redevelopment.

Another wizard born in Carmarthen is Matthew Stevens. Matthew is a magician on the snooker table and it's only a matter of time before he becomes World Champion.

With the bike safely stowed in Geraint's garage, I took a shower and changed into clean clothes. Over a cup of tea or two, I recounted my journey to date. Geraint was particularly interested in the Aberaeron episode, naturally, because of his family connections with the town.

We dined in the conservatory. Pauline, Geraint's wife, prepared pasta for all of us, but with a very nice vegetarian sauce for me. Post pasta we had biscuits and a delicious blue vein cheese which they'd brought back from their recent holiday to Italy. After another hard day's ride, I was so hungry that I'm ashamed to say I ate a huge quantity of biscuits and polished off the Italian cheese as well.

When you get to my age, you know everything. The hard part is trying to remember it. That's why I taped the following conversation with Geraint :-

JD: "How does Carmarthen compare now to when you first moved here?"

GG: "I think Carmarthen probably reflects similar changes that have happened all over the world really. When I came to Carmarthen 30 years ago, you couldn't even buy a bulb of garlic here. Well now you can get pretty much anything you need. The town has changed. It's more prosperous now, the population has grown, but I don't think it's changed its character. You get more day trippers, more tourism. One of the major changes, especially over the last five or ten years, is the amount of immigrants, from England mainly. There are new shops and new housing projects and yet the nature of Carmarthen hasn't changed much. You don't have to be in Carmarthen long before you go native. In essence, Carmarthen is still a small, Welsh county town with its atmosphere and character still largely intact."

JD: "Are the changes for the better or worse?"

GG: "Carmarthen has changed for the better I would say. Education and health care have improved. Access to the outside world has improved. Carmarthen had 5% unemployment when I came here first and I think it's the same now. The main reason for Carmarthen's existence, except for protecting the lowest crossing point of the River Tywi, is agriculture and that's still the case. Overall, I think Carmarthen is still a good place to live and a good place to bring up children. It's still a safe, friendly town. I would say that it has pretty much maintained its atmosphere and character over the last 30 years, miraculously."

JD: "What's the best thing about living in Carmarthen?"

GG: "Depends on what you want. Carmarthen has got very good restaurants, a swimming pool, cinema and three theatres. It's got beautiful beaches nearby. Pendine and Cefn Sidan are remarkable beaches. It's got a wealth of heritage and history. I've been to Tuscany and the Dordogne many times on holidays. It's ironic that I go to places that are very similar to Carmarthenshire, albeit there's a little bit more sunshine. Carmarthen has a wonderful mix of sea, mountain and rolling hills. The appeal of Carmarthen is that it has all these natural resources and countryside. It's a most beautiful place to live."

JD: "What's the worst thing about living in Carmarthen?"

GG: "There's no such thing as a perfect place. Perfection doesn't exist, but it's a lot of fun trying to attain it. Would I want to criticise Carmarthen? No, not really. I live here because I chose it out of many potential places to live. It suits me and it's the kind of town you can get very fond of. It's got a nice balance. Are there disadvantages to living in Carmarthen? Not one I could particularly dwell on. There are certainly worse places to live in the world and that's the truth?"

JD: "What's the best thing about being a professional artiste and musician?"

GG: "If you can achieve the situation whereby you're paid to do what you love doing, you're very blessed. Most people have to do what they're prepared to put up with. If you're an artiste you're living a dream. If you can sustain yourself whilst doing it, it's brilliant. Nobody can ask more than to be allowed to indulge themselves in what they enjoy doing and get paid for it. You don't have to do other stuff that gets in the way, like a day job. You're very privileged if you can do it. I wish that I was paid more mind."

JD: "What kind of music do you listen to now?"

GG: "When I go on holidays, I take a small MP3 player with me. What I put on it is quite telling really. Ry Cooder, Paul Brady, Davy Spillane, Tom Waits. Often stuff from the 70s and 80s. I'm still listening to music I've been listening to all of my life, but I do listen to new stuff. Like the Dixie Chicks for instance, just off the top of my head. I buy an album and I can normally spot the influences. I'll think perhaps it's very 'Beatley' or very 'Byrdy'. There's a lot of recycling that goes on. There's nothing wrong with that. As long as the words are good, the harmonies are nice, the guitar work is interesting and it's not over produced. I'm still listening now to the kind of stuff I was listening to 20 years ago and enjoying it."

JD: "What do you think of the new modern footbridge that crosses the river to the station?"

GG: "There has been an ongoing, extensive and tedious debate about the footbridge. I like it. When you walk west along Quay Street you can see the bridge's white-painted vertical supports. It looks as if there's a masted ship at anchor at the quay. A view that was once very common in Wales' oldest town and indeed in Wales' biggest and busiest port, pre industrial revolution."

JD: "Are you still thinking of moving to Ireland?"

GG: "My mother was one of the reasons why I felt I could never leave Carmarthen. Before she died we stayed close by to support her. My work is mainly television drama, radio drama, writing and recording. The writing and recording I can certainly do in Ireland. The acting work I can only do in Wales. I would never want to leave here completely because this is where I belong. It's from this place that I get my perspective on everything else. It's very much a Welsh perspective. I'd miss this place, the people, my friends, my family, and my world - the Welsh world, the Welsh language world. My work and indeed ninety percent of my life is conducted in the Welsh language. I'd miss that. It would be nice to spend the winter in the South of France and come back here for the summer, but that's not a realistic possibility. No, I think I'll settle for Carmarthen. I'll stay here, thank you very much."

Geraint likes technological gadgetry. He'd taken photos of their holiday in Tuscany with his digital camera and edited them on to a DVD. He'd then added backing music by Irish musician Davy Spillane. The still photos appeared on the TV screen so seamlessly that it gave the impression of being a moving picture.

We spent the remainder of the evening reminiscing on old times. As we chatted, Geraint's cat joined us. He's black and white and very friendly. As he settled down for a nap, an odd thought crossed my mind - do cats suffer from insomnia? This one certainly didn't.

The slight irregularity I suffered in my bowels in the morning had been ok all day. As the evening wore on my stomach started making some ominous gurgling noises. Fortunately, the Griffiths family doesn't stay up late. I made a sharp exit for the toilet to release my discomfort and then headed happily to bed.

# Monday, 19th June

*There was an old man from Port Talbot*

*While cycling round Wales hit a wall but*

*Just jiggled and joggled*

*And wibbled and wobbled*

*Till getting back home to Port Talbot*

On this day in 1937 the author of 'Peter Pan', J. M. Barrie, died; in 1947 Salman Rushdie was born; in 1964 Boris Johnson, MP for Henley on Thames, was born; in 1965 Tambourine Man by The Byrds hit No.1; in 1981 the heaviest orange ever was weighed in at 2.5 Kg in Nelspruit, South Africa.

Slept quite well and woke at 6.45am. I had decided long before leaving on this trip that I wouldn't run when I stayed at Geraint's. I didn't want to inconvenience them with my weird ways. Besides which, there was that hell of a hill to climb back up to the house.

Pauline was working. I heard her get up and she left for work at 7.45 by which time I needed to go to the toilet again. The problem was improving, you'll be glad to hear. I was glad anyway.

Geraint wasn't up yet so I flicked through the paper while waiting for him. One headline caught my eye. It said, 'Equality of the sexes leaves women standing on buses'. It's quite true too. There was a time in my youth when I would never let a lady stand on a bus. I caught the park'n'ride bus into Swansea last week. There must have been a dozen women standing while I sat, as did a couple of other men. I didn't feel comfortable about it mind.

Geraint surfaced soon after. He made us breakfast of freshly squeezed orange juice, followed by his own recipe for porridge. He buys oranges by the boxfull. To the oats he added - golden linseed, wheat germ, pecan nuts, blueberries, maple syrup and honey. It was fine fodder for a starving cyclist.

It seems as though honey is the only food that never spoils. I read somewhere that a pot of honey was found in an Egyptian tomb. The archaeologists tried it and it was still edible after thousands of years.

We had an interesting discussion about the relative values of language and the education system over breakfast. Our children were taught that the content of an essay is more important than punctuation and spelling. Geraint tended to agree with this. I maintain that you've got to have uniform punctuation and spelling so that everyone interprets a sentence in the same way. It was a heavyweight topic for breakfast, but it didn't affect my digestion at all.

Then it was time to leave. Before I left, Geraint checked my bike over. He inflated my tyres to a solid 80lbs/sq.in. and replaced an inner tube valve nut which I hadn't noticed was missing. We said our goodbyes and I set off through Carmarthen in cool, cloudy conditions.

I was soon pedalling past Mynydd y Garreg, home of ex Welsh rugby international, Ray Gravell. He is now a very enthusiastic and entertaining presenter on Radio Cymru and S4C.

By the time I got to Kidwelly, it was raining (That sounds like a good first line for a song!). Only a shower which soon passed. I've been to Kidwelly Castle once, a long time ago. I didn't call in this time, even though it's a magnificent sight. It was significantly altered over hundreds of years by its many owners, but eventually fell into disrepair.

I flew past Pembrey on a long, straight stretch of road. It wasn't worth stopping because Pembrey has only got a country park, cross country course, dry ski slope, links golf course, motor racing circuit, airport, eight mile blue flag beach and a marina at nearby Burry Port. Apart from that there's nothing there.

There were no pigs in the pig field in Pembrey either. On my regular trips to run in the country park, I have to pass a large field by the side of the main road. This has always been occupied by a herd of pigs who have turned it into a huge mud wallow.

The story I heard was that the owner of the field requested planning permission to build houses there. The neighbours objected and planning permission was denied. It then became a muddy pig field instead of nice new houses being built there. No houses, and no pigs this time. The field was already looking greener. I wonder if a pig lost its voice would it be dis-grunt-led.

Onward and into Llanelli. I could write a book about Llanelli alone. Somebody's already done it though, I think. Industry played a major part in Llanelli's development into a town of significance. By the end of the 19th century it was nicknamed 'Tinopolis' because of the huge tonnage of tinplate produced there.

You can't write about Llanelli and not mention Stradey Park and the Scarlets. I can't anyway. There's been a proud tradition of rugby in Llanelli since 1872. There have been many famous players and many famous victories like the one in 1972 against New Zealand when the pubs ran dry.

On my way to Cardiff to see the Welsh Cup Final in 1976, I overtook a Scarlets supporters' bus. In the back window of the bus a banner proclaimed, 'Scarlets Annual Outing'. That day was their fourth cup final victory in as many years.

The A484 out of Llanelli is quite flat. Although the traffic was heavy and there was another light shower, it didn't take long to reach Gowerton, the Gateway to the Gower. From coal to steel and even a pickled onion factory, Gowerton was at one time a heavily industrialised town. The industry is no more. There wasn't the slightest scent of ascetic as I cycled through.

When my Mam took me to Swansea market many years ago, we would never leave without a punnet of Penclawdd cockles and half a pound of laver bread. The cockles were gathered by women with donkey carts in those days. Today, it's a male dominated industry using tractors.

Between Crofty and Llanrhidian, there was a grassy area alongside a junction where I took a break. The grass was a bit damp, but there was a concrete triangle in the middle of it which was dry enough to sit on. The Llanrhidian Holiday Camp was on the landward side of the road. I sat facing the estuary with a view back towards Llanelli and Burry Port.

Before I actually sat down, a small grey horse trotted across the field and hung his head over the hedge. Oh no, here we go again, I thought, another audience while I eat. Not this time though. He soon lost interest, started nibbling at the hedge, then moved off. Soon after, I moved off.

Just beyond Oldwalls is Weobley Castle which isn't a castle at all. It was built as a fortified manor house in the 14th century by the de la Bere family. Miss Emily Charlotte Mansel Talbot, who once lived just up the road from me, donated it to the forerunner of CADW in 1911. I never knew her personally, mind. I'm not that old.

An exhilarating downhill dash, then through a narrow lane past the Fairyhill Hotel. What happens after you go downhill? You have to go up again. I bumped across a cattle grid, then toiled to the top of Cefn Bryn Common. It was worth it for the view across the Rhossili Downs to the sea.

The beautiful land and seascapes of the Gower Peninsula have been preserved thanks to its being designated Britain's first Area of Outstanding Natural Beauty. In fact, in May of this year (2006) the Gower celebrates its 50th anniversary as an AONB.

What happens when you go up hill? You've got to go down again. I missed my bike computer here. The road down off the common was relatively straight. I must have been close to 100mph. Well, it felt like it anyway, but I'll never know now.

From the common, I rode down through Lunnon. The descent was so steep, narrow and winding that I had to keep the brakes on all the way down. I came out by Shepherd's Store at the bottom and headed for Bishopston. Going east, I came to West Cross on the seafront at Swansea Bay.

When I was in junior school, our teacher told us about the Red Lady of Paviland. This was a skeleton found buried in Paviland Cave on the Gower. It was discovered in 1823 when they thought it to be female because of the necklaces and ornaments buried with it. The skeleton was red because the body had been covered in red ochre before burial. Our teacher didn't tell us that they also thought she was a Roman prostitute. I found that out later.

Modern techniques have established that it was actually a man not a woman and probably of some tribal importance, hence the artifacts buried with him. He probably lived 29,000 years ago making this the oldest burial to be found in Britain. A skeleton was found during the renovation of a barn down the road from us. There was no identification, just a medallion around its neck with the inscription, 'Hide and Seek Champion - 1935'.

Geraint Davies' father was from Machynlleth and his mother was from the Rhondda. Geraint was born in Merthyr. What has this to do with my cycle ride and Swansea you ask? Geraint has lived in Swansea, except for a few years in Aberystwyth, since 1963. He is the co-author and translator of my last book.

Geraint has worked as a BBC Radio Cymru producer and is also an accomplished guitarist and harmony singer. He was a founder member of Welsh language band Hergest. He has written many songs over the last 30 years while playing with 'Mynediad Am Ddim' who still perform on a part time basis. We met at his home in Craigcefnparc a couple of weeks before my journey where I recorded this conversation:-

JD: "Where did you spend your early years?"

GD: "I was born in Merthyr in 1953 and lived in Nelson till I was three. We lived in Llandovery till I was 10, then moved to

Bonymaen. At that time it was a fairly small area, a Welsh speaking area and not half as rough as it is today."

JD: "Have you always been a Welsh speaker?"

GD: "My father was a minister. His background is totally Welsh speaking. My mother not so much really. So we were brought up bilingually, I would say."

JD: "Did you go to a Welsh speaking school?"

GD: "I think the early years in Llandovery were bilingual. They had a Welsh wing as part of the school. When we moved to Swansea I went to my only year of Welsh language education in Llansamlet. I hated that year. Then I went through the 11+. Swansea was an interesting case at that time. It had gone semi comprehensive. I had the choice of going to Penlan Comprehensive or one of the two grammar schools, Bishop Gore and Dinefwr, which were both single sex. I opted to go to Dinefwr. It didn't have as much tradition as Bishop Gore, but it was slap bang in the middle of Town, which suited me. For the next seven years I was educated in Dinefwr and spent my lunch hour roaming town, around the shops and eating in cafes. The building was almost like a prison block. Three side of a quadrangle and in the middle a yard. The playing fields were up in Town Hill, a bus ride away."

JD: "Did you like sport?"

GD: "No, I was hopeless. I suffered from asthma quite badly, so pushing myself athletically was not a great attraction. You got on a service bus to go up to games on Town Hill. A lot of us would go up there, check in, check nobody was looking, then catch the next bus back to town. From about Form 3 on I was absent continually. I've got to a stage now where I take medication for my blood pressure. The nurse tells me to go walking, but it's almost an alien thing."

JD: "Have you always had an interest in music?"

GD: "Music was always in the family. My mother played piano and she was chapel organist. I was given piano lessons. I think

I've always been resistant to anything given to me. I wasn't all that keen, there was a little rebel in me coming out. Then my piano teacher had a breakdown. I've been told there's no connection. I said I wouldn't mind having a go at the violin. I did it up to o-level, by that time I wanted a guitar. The deal was to do my grade 5 and they'd buy me a guitar. I haven't touched a violin since."

JD: "What were your early musical influences?"

GD: "Seven years old, on a Saturday night in Llandovery, I fell in love with pop music. It was a John Leyton song called 'Wild Wind'. The first two records I bought were by Barry McGuire, 'Eve of Destruction' and the follow up 'Precious Time'. My father had been writing lyrics and a few tunes, so the Morriston Urdd asked me to write lyrics and translate a few things. I was doing Welsh in Form 6 by then. There was a group of girls singing in Welsh called 'Yr Awr' (The Hour). They asked me to translate Red Rubber Ball, a Paul Simon song. It was recorded, my first recorded work. It still irks Delwyn Sion now, that there's a record credit that says Paul Simon/Geraint Davies, because Paul Simon is his big hero. Then we fell out, the band and me. It was '69. They took part in a concert as part of the Investiture celebrations (Charles, Prince of Wales). Well I wasn't up for the Investiture celebrations."

JD: "Are you a Welsh Nationalist?"

GD: "Absolutely, a Welsh Nationalist. My nationalism is very much rooted in the language. I'm not, I hope, an elitist. It's not that I've got no time for non Welsh speakers or that I don't believe that non Welsh speakers are not Welsh. Most of my interests are non Welsh speaking."

JD: "Your first band was Welsh speaking though"

GD: "A mate of mine from Swansea was on the same course as me. We came back and started our first little band. We added a girl playing mandolin and guitar, she sang as well, and a bongo player and that was us. We were called 'Gwenwyn', (Poison).

Very heavy name for a very lightweight band. It was all acoustic, very folky. We were writing our own material and we got a record deal, made a couple of EPs."

JD: "How did you become a BBC producer?"

GD: "Did my degree in Welsh, decided to be a teacher, hated it. Got a job with the Urdd working for the Eisteddfod. Then got another job with the Urdd as a kind of language officer for about two and a half years. Then I got a phone call, out of the blue, from Bryn Jones, a producer with the BBC. They were opening a radio studio in Swansea and they were looking for more people. He asked whether I'd be interested in trying. So I tried for it and was lucky enough to get it."

JD: "Has your work always been in the Welsh language?"

GD: "Exclusively. I've worked with a lot of presenters, given them a little nudge on. Quite a few people did their first radio work with me on Radio Cymru. People like Elinor Jones, Dai Jones Llanilar and Ray Gravell. I worked with Aled Samuel on Sunday afternoon. It was Aled Sam playing records and we thought we'd do a bit of reading from the Sunday papers. We got Dafydd Bevan in. Dafydd is brilliant in his own right. He's just a funny cynical guy. We'd get there Sunday morning with all the papers, sit around finding stupid stuff. We'd go out, have a liquid lunch, get back and they'd get the giggles very often. There was one story that Dafydd had found, about the German Husband of the Year. He'd been arrested for killing his wife. He battered her to death with his trophy. This is not a funny story really, but they started giggling and they couldn't stop. So, we go into a record, we come out of the record and they're still giggling. They'd just gone west."

JD: "Do you like modern music?"

GD: "There was a stage when I refused to listen to anybody younger than me. I'm not quite that bad now. Some of the new stuff is the same as the old stuff. Have you heard of the Storys? We know where they're coming from. I'm still a sucker for that kind of stuff. My heroes tend to be the same. Crosby, Stills, Nash and Young; The Byrds; Gram Parsons; Gene Clark. I think rock'n'roll, as a genre, has run its course anyway. There's nothing new. Nothing much has changed in the last 50 years really."

JD: "What's your opinion of Swansea?"

GD: "I've lived here more than half my life. I was wise enough, even at the age of 10, to say it'll be nice when they finish it. The Germans made a hell of a dent and the planners have made almost as big a hash of it since. It's been interesting to see how the centre of town has been gravitating towards the sea from the station. There's nothing in High Street now, it's derelict. Perpetual construction and it's not getting anywhere. So Dylan Thomas had it just about right, this ugly, lovely town. Nobody, or very few people live in the centre of Swansea. It's not particularly residential. The city divides the community."

JD: "Would you move out of Swansea, say back to Llandovery, if you could?"

GD: "My wife is a Morriston girl, but I would. I had this thing, almost a calling to go back to Llandovery. A spiritual thing. I spook my wife sometimes with these thoughts or premonitions. I'm a sceptic on most things, but as you get older and crankier you start to believe them. My mentor in Llandovery junior school was my teacher, Kathryn Ann Preece. Apart from my parents, she was the biggest influence of my life, looking back. She was totally dedicated, loved literature and writing. She got me writing and performing. So, I'll go and see her. She's in her 80s and in a home. She was a bit befuddled and it took a while, but then she knew me. She was very tearful when I left. She died three days later. It was a good day, strange, but I'm so glad I went. I hope it wasn't me who sent her off."

To my right was Mumbles, home of Hollywood superstar Katherine Zeta Jones and sensational singer Bonnie Tyler. I crossed the road and turned left onto the seafront cycle track which was once the Swansea to Mumbles Tramway. Construction began in 1804. In 1897 it became the first railway line in the world to operate a passenger service. By 1929, the steam trains had been replaced by electric tramcars which I remember riding a couple of times in the late 50s. Regretfully, the line was closed down in 1960. What a tourist draw that would have been now.

Before we leave the Gower completely, there was another story Mr. Jones the teacher told us all those years ago in school. This is how I remember it - A Gower farmer was woken one night by the sound of music coming from the barn where he kept his prize bull. He put on his shoes and coat and peeped in through the barn window where he saw dozens of pixies. The pixies, dressed in green and red clothes, were singing and dancing to the sweet sound of seven violins. The farmer found that he could neither speak nor move as more pixies arrived.

Suddenly the music stopped. The pixies slaughtered the bull and feasted on it until only the bones and hide were left. After the feast they put all the bones back together, except for one bone missing from the left hind foot. Despite a desperate search the bone could not be found. Daylight was fast approaching so the pixies quickly sewed the bull's hide back on. To the farmer's amazement, the beast clambered to its feet and started feeding as if nothing had happened.

The farmer remembered nothing then till he woke in bed the next day, thinking he'd had a bad dream. After breakfast, he let the bull out of the barn and as it walked across the farmyard, he saw that it was limping on its left hind leg.

A brief stop to recharge the batteries opposite Swansea University, where writer Kingsley Amis taught for many years. Then I rejoined the main road at the end of the cycle track. As I passed through the familiar sights of Swansea, it dawned on me that I would soon be home -

And back with the little gem in my life

The two carat diamond that is my dear wife.

It was quite an emotional experience and brought a lump to my throat. Another shower soon put a damper on that though.

Up and over the old Briton Ferry Bridge and down into Baglan - Port Talbot at last.

What can I say that hasn't been said about Port Talbot already. It's an industrial wasteland of fire-breathing flare pipes, chain smoking chimneys and chemical quicksands. It's home though. These things aren't as bad as they used to be either. BP chemicals, where I worked for 30 years, has gone. The Margam coke ovens have gone. It's a lot cleaner than it used to be when Max Boyce joked that people from Port Talbot couldn't tell the difference between the sun and the moon because they'd never seen them.

Never mind the sun and moon. What about the stars. Richard Burton, Anthony Hopkins, Michael Sheen, Ivor Emmanuel, Rebecca Evans, Rob Brydon, Geraint Griffiths, Chris Needs. There must be something good in the air there.

The Romans don't seem to have settled in Aberafan as it was originally called. There were only a few hovels near the mouth of the River Afan when the Normans arrived in 1090. Margam Abbey was founded in 1137, then a stone castle was built in the village in 1153. There are no visible remains of this castle now.

Henry VIII dissolved the monasteries in 1535 and Sir Rice Mansel of Gower bought Margam Abbey and its lands for £2494/13s/5d. From about 1700 onwards the industrialization of the Aberafan district began with collieries, copper, iron and tin works.

Christopher Rice Mansel Talbot inherited the Margam Estate in 1824. He was responsible for developing the harbour at Aberafan and it was named Port Talbot in his honour. In 1851, the longest rail in Britain (62foot 5inches) was made in Cwmafan for the Crystal Palace Exhibition.

The various parts of the steel works were established during the 20th century, but it's been downhill for many years now. All the heavy industry has disappeared, except for a reduced steel works which is a shadow of its former self.

Phoned Ad at work as soon as I got in to tell her I was home safely. Had some tea and toast, unpacked the bike then showered and changed. Even if you stay in five star luxury, there's no place like home. It seemed like ages and yet the previous 10 days had passed in a blur.

I'm the chief cook and bottle washer in our house, so I set to work on a vegetarian spaghetti Bolognese. Ad is not a veggie, but I can tempt her with my culinary craft occasionally. My secret is a glass of good red wine with everything I cook. Not in the food, I drink it.

That's the longest we've ever been apart and our reunion was joyful to say the least. During the meal, I caught up on all the news in between reminiscences of my bike journey.

We lived in an old semi detached house in the centre of Port Talbot for 26 years. Ad always wanted a brand new house, so we moved to our present home in the suburb of Margam in December 2000.

We are lucky to have a lovely couple living next door. Sian has stuck with her surname of Orrells because of her script writing career. Her husband, Frank Watkins, took early retirement from teaching to care for Sian who suffers from multiple sclerosis. Frank taught art and is himself a talented artist with several prizes and exhibitions to his name.

Multiple sclerosis is an inflammatory disease of the brain and spinal chord. Lesions form on the nerve cells causing the loss of voluntary and involuntary movements in most sufferers. There are different types of the disease and it's usually progressive. This is only a simplified explanation of a very complex condition.

I didn't have to go very far to record this conversation with Sian and Frank:-

JD: "You were born in Port Talbot, Sian?"

Sian: "Yes, I was. Neath General Hospital to be exact, but raised in Port Talbot. We lived in London for a year and 15 years in Cardiff. Then we moved here to Margam three years ago."

Frank: "I was born in Glanamman."

JD: "You both spent some time away in college as well did you?"

Sian: "I went to Aberystwyth first. Then I swapped to go to Swansea Institute of Higher Education. That's where I actually got my degree from. I started doing Drama at Aberystwyth and I just hated it up there. So I moved to Swansea and had a whale of a time."

Frank: "After school, I went to Carmarthen Art School for a year's foundation course. Then I went to Newport Art College for three years and a year teacher training. All told, I taught for 22 years in different places. My first three years were here in Port Talbot, in Dyffryn."

JD: "So you came out with an art degree, did you?"

Frank: "Graphic Design actually. The summer I finished college, I started painting. I'd only drawn before that. That's more or less when it started seriously. I've always painted since then."

Sian: "I did honours in Art History and English."

JD: "How did you become a script writer then?"

Sian: "That's what I do. I don't really know. I entered a competition actually. The Radio Times Award in 1990. I wrote a script for that and got second place, which I thought at the time was really good. Then I saw the winners script and I thought I can do better than this. So I got an agent and she got me on to programmes like 'Eastenders', which I did for a few years. Then 'Inspector Wycliffe', I did a few of those. After that it was 'Touching Evil' and 'Touch of Frost'. Then I did my own series for BBC Wales called 'Jack of Hearts'. I've had no work for the last five or six years though. I changed my agent a couple of months ago, because my original agent has given up on me."

JD: "Why has your agent given up on you?"

Sian: "It's because I can't get to London at the drop of a hat. So I've got a new agent who's very good. She's going to get me on a series called 'The Street'. I'm waiting to hear from the producer, Andrew McGovern. So that's my career for you. I wrote a script for the Drama Awards and realized it was something I could do."

JD: "Have you always been interested in art Frank?"

Frank: "Yes, all my life really. It was just something I could do and I was always interested in reading about artists. The first art book I bought with my pocket money as a kid was the 'Readers Digest of Great Painters and Paintings' which I've still got."

JD: "Have you got a painting hero?"

Frank: "Yes, I've got a few. There are certain artists I never tire of looking at. People like Antoni Tapies, Joseph Boyce, Giacometti, Kurt Schwitters and Morandi. I'm sort of interested in all kinds of art, but these people I always go back to. I just love their work."

JD: "What do you call the type of work that you do?"

Frank: "I don't think you can slot it into a category. I don't paint in a conventional way. I use all sorts of things, it's mixed media painting. I guess they're abstract, but there are figurative aspects as well. The work I do is mainly colourless. I don't mean black and white. They're non-colours if you like. You won't find any bright colours in my work, they're just sort of browns. That makes them not always accessible to people. In this day and age people want colour, they want a quick fix. You've got to give my work a lot of time. It sort of grows on people."

JD: "Would you like to have been a professional artist, although most of them died before they became famous didn't they?"

Frank: "That's a bit of a myth. There are millions of very famous artists who make an awful lot of money at it. You've got to be doing a certain type of work and you've got to be in the right place."

Sian: "That's what I was going to say. It would help both of us if we were in the right place at the right time."

Frank: "Wales is not the right place. People don't appreciate art as such. I think you've got to be in a bigger place, a big city like London."

JD: "Have you written anything else, Sian, apart from scripts?"

Sian: "No. I started writing a book, but it's sort of died for a while now because my interest has moved to another script I'm going to write. It's very difficult to write a book and a script when your instincts tell you to write a script. To write a book is totally different."

JD: "Do you write dialogue in a script like you would in a book?"

Sian: "No. You imagine a story. Say it's a programme like 'Frost'. you imagine what could happen to the character. Then you'd write various scenes of how he'd go about doing things. That just comes naturally to me."
  JD: "Have you got a writing hero?"

Sian: "No, not really. Writers I admire. People like Jimmy McGovern. I like some American novelists. People like Raymond Chandler who used to write good whodunits."

JD: "Do you have to do a lot of research?"

Sian: "I don't do any research. I read books. Many of the ideas come out of something from a book and I'll think I could put that in a script."

JD: "Do you mind talking about your multiple sclerosis?"

Sian: "No, carry on, I don't mind. I used to hate doing it, but now I don't mind. I don't care who knows."

Frank: "At the start no one knew you had it because you used to get about normally."

Sian: "Dr. Weiser diagnosed it in 1989. I'd had a brain scan. That was like sticking your head in a washing machine. Not a very nice experience. It didn't hurt at all, it's just that it was quite frightening. I saw him the following week and he said you've got MS. I just laughed because I didn't know what it was. I felt ok in myself, so I just laughed and thought thank God it's not cancer. He said at the moment it's ok, but give it eight or nine years, then it will hit you. And so I'm like this now, having to use a wheelchair."

Frank; "It was an optician who told you to go for more tests."

Sian: "Optic neuritis, that's where it started. I thought I needed a new pair of glasses. Things seemed very blurred. After doing the eye test he said you'd better see a neurologist. So I made the appointment to see Dr. Weiser and you know the rest."

JD: "Does it affect your work?"

Sian: "No. I suffer because I can't get about to meetings and stuff."

JD: "Have you met any of the actors who have performed your scripts?"

Sian: "I've met piles. I met David Jason and all the other actors in 'Frost' and all the characters in everything I've written. Except for 'Eastenders', you don't meet anyone for that. It's just another person, I don't treat anybody differently than I always do. I've never met anybody who puts on airs and graces. I've met some awkward beggars, but I won't tell you who they are. As for the future, I'll just carry on."

JD: "What are your plans for the future, Frank?"

Frank: "I've got an exhibition next month in the new gallery in Penarth called Oriel Tree. If I was doing landscapes and vases of flowers, things like that which people readily take to, I might have a lot more work, but that's not what I choose to do and I'm ready to accept that."

JD: "What's your opinion of Port Talbot?"

Frank: "I rarely go into town. As a town I don't particularly like it. I think it's boring. I think the architecture, the things the council have put up, is disgraceful. Aberafan House in the town centre I think is the ugliest building in the country. And you can't park anywhere. There are yellow lines everywhere. There isn't anywhere left in Wales now where you can park just anywhere. I think a lot of it is to do with the way that supermarkets have taken over. When you have large supermarkets in small towns they tend to be in the centre, like here and Ammanford and Neath. Then you have such a volume of traffic you have to change the outline of the small towns. You don't get that so much in cities. A lot of people have this negative view of Port Talbot because of the industry. The steel works is so vast, they think of Port Talbot and that's what they think of. I think Port Talbot suffers the way every town in Wales suffers and councillors have a very narrow vision. Anything that's old, they'll knock it down and put up something that they think is wonderful. It's just crap, pseudo architecture. I like the areas outside of Port Talbot, like Pontrhydyfen and Cwmafan. I like this area, especially where we are here. We've got Margam Park behind us and we're not far from the sea. It's nice."

JD: "Do you have any hobbies?"

Frank: "Reading, books. I like Samuel Becket, James Elroy, Ian Rankin. We read the same books, thrillers. We came across this Icelandic writer. Very good. They've only translated two of his books into English so far. His name is Arnaldur Indridason."

Sian: "Work and football, Liverpool. I remember seeing the FA Cup Final in 1974 and they beat Newcastle. That was the day it clicked with me, that this was my team and I've stayed with them ever since. I've been to Anfield a couple of times with my father."

JD: "If you had a free choice where would you live?"

Frank: "Abroad, anywhere."

Sian: "The States. I've been to New York a few times, but I wouldn't really want to go back there. Somewhere on the West Coast."

Frank: "It's not going to happen."

Sian: "No, dream on."

I was home, yes, but the journey wasn't over yet. I still had to get to Chepstow to complete the trip that I'd planned. I find TV very educational. Normally, when it's switched on I go and read a book. The panniers had to be packed though, so I spent part of the evening digging out clean clothes and kit ready for the morning. Then, breaking with tradition, I chilled out with an ice cold lager for an hour's viewing before bed.

# Tuesday, 20th June

*There was a young lady from Chepstow*
*Who let the nails on her big toes grow*
*They got longer and longer*
*And bigger and stronger*
*Till the ends ended up in Old Bairstow*

On this day in 451 Theodred King of the Visigoths died; in 1837 Victoria became Queen of Britain; in 1909 actor Errol Flynn was born; in 1942 Brian Wilson of The Beachboys was born.

Lately I've been spending a lot of time thinking about the here after. I go somewhere to get something, then when I get there wonder what I'm here after. That was certainly the case when I walked into the kitchen on the morning of the final leg of my journey from Chester to Chepstow.

I'd already been up for a couple of hours. During that time, I'd been for a run, showered, dressed and had breakfast. I stood in the kitchen for a puzzled moment, then it came to me. The bike computer. I'd forgotten it when I left home the first time. This time it was going with me. I took it from the draw where it's kept and fixed it to the bike.

I was just putting the finishing touches to the preparations when Ian arrived. The son who'd started me off on this journey was going to accompany me on the last stage. To my surprise, he was riding his girlfriend, Tina's, bike. His reasoning became obvious when he pointed out that Tina's bike was a hybrid and more suitable for the road. It's an Apollo Crosstrack with Shimano SIG derailleur and Gripstaff Max gear change. The most important items were the tyres. They were a hybrid type, not too wide and not too heavily treaded. This meant less resistance to the road and an easier ride for Ian.

His own bike is an out and out American off roader. It's a Klein Karma with front and rear suspension, Shimano Deore LX derailleur and SRAM Attack grip twist gear change. The tyres are huge, knobbly WTB Velociraptors. They're almost like motorbike tyres. There were no panniers on the Apollo, so I packed Ian's overnight stuff into mine and we left just after 9 am.

There's no word for weather in the Hawaiian language. Probably because they have to suffer so much sunshine all the time. There was no sunshine in South Wales. It was cool and cloudy as we pedalled from Port Talbot.

From North Cornelly, we took the A48 bypassing the seaside resort of Porthcawl with its famous Trecco Bay caravan park. We left the main road at Merthyr Mawr, an idyllic little village with thatched roof cottages. Between the village and the sea are some of the biggest sand dunes you'll ever see. The 'Big Dipper' is reckoned to be the biggest dune in Europe and some scenes from 'Lawrence of Arabia' were shot in this area. A number of noted runners like Steve Ovett have used these dunes for training. I've run up the Big Dipper once and that was enough for me.

We crossed the Ogmore river by way of the 15th century 'Dipping Bridge'. It's a narrow stone bridge with holes in its walls through which the sheep were pushed for a death-defying dip in the water below.

Pottery has been turned in Ewenny since the 15th century. The Ewenny Pottery is remarkable in that it's the oldest working pottery in Wales. Caitlin Jenkins is the ninth generation of the same family to run the business.

We kept pottering on into Wick. It's a small village with a big claim to fame in cycling circles. My biking heroine, Nicole Cooke, was born in Wick in 1983. She's won too many titles to list and should have been chosen as the Sports Personality of this year after winning the World Championship.

Our Ian has enjoyed cycling from a very early age. I was washing my car in the back lane one day while he rode up and down on his little bike. It was a two wheeler with stabilizers at the back. He did this a few times then shouted to me, "Daddy, Daddy, take the stabilizers off". He was only three and a half at the time. I hesitated for a moment then I thought, why not? So off they came and off he went without a wobble. He took to it like the proverbial amphibious military vehicle to liquefied steam. Ian has always been a keen cyclist since then, though like his Dad, not on the competitive side.

*No time for Wick*

*To get on our wick*

*And no saint was sager*

*Than Illtud of Major*

Illtud was born in Brittany in the 6th century. He came to Wales as a soldier, then turning to religion, founded the Abbey of Llanilltud Fawr (Llantwit Major) in the Vale of Glamorgan. He was an intelligent and eloquent man whose monastic school attracted pupils like Baglan, Gildas and David. They were all sainted and David became the Patron Saint of Wales.

The spinning wheels of our cycles safely carried us past Llantwit Major, but before we leave the Bridgend district, there's one more interview to recount.

Dafydd James, Welsh Rugby International and British Lion, was not born in Bridgend, but does regard it as his home town. He currently plays for the Scarlets Regional Team and is a neighbour of mine. We train together on the local playing fields, or perhaps I should say we're often training on the fields at the same time. He's probably not quite as quick as me - over 10Km. This conversation was recorded in my home :-

JD: "You weren't born in Wales were you?"

DJ: "I was born in Zambia. My parents were working out there. My Dad was in the copper mines and we lived there a couple of years before we came back to Wales. My older brother was born in Bridgend, so the family are all from Bridgend originally."

JD: "Where did you live after Zambia?"

DJ: "I was brought up in Bridgend, in Brackla. We stayed there for a few years before moving to South Africa. My sister was born in South Africa. Then we came back to Wales and we've been here ever since."

JD: "Would you call Bridgend your home town?"

DJ: "That's where I lived the majority of my life, so I suppose, yes."

JD: "Who did you play rugby for in your younger days?"

DJ: "I played for Bridgend Schools Under 15s and after that I was with Cornelly Youth. My family are from Cornelly and Kenfig Hill, so then I played for Kenfig Hill. I was fortunate to move to Bridgend where my career seemed to take off really."

JD: "You know Bridgend quite well then?"

DJ: "Fairly well, yes. It's an old town, probably needs a bit of revamping now. New bridge Fields is a nice part where you can train and get out for a walk in the summer. Merthyr Mawr is a fantastic place with all the sand dunes."

JD: "What inspired you to play rugby in the first place?"

DJ: "My Dad played rugby at an early age, but got injured and his mother and grandmother wouldn't allow him to play, so he played football. He was a keen footballer actually. Then, when he moved to Zambia, he started to play rugby again. He played in South Africa and he played over here as well. As me and my brother were growing up we used to go and watch him play. Just watching him really, and it went from there. As young children in South Africa we did a lot of athletics because, obviously, the climate's a lot better. Played a little bit of rugby with my brother. There was only 18 months between us, so we were always pushing each other."

JD: "With your height, did you ever consider playing as a forward?"

DJ: "No. I first played when I was six, I think. I started off in the front row - hooker. I played one game there. That was enough, I was out of there rapidly. I considered it when I was in Youth, but I stayed in my position and went on to have Welsh Youth honours, so I was glad I didn't change."

JD: "Did you have a rugby hero in those days?"

DJ: "Yes, Phil Bennet and Gareth Edwards. As I got a bit older Jonathan Davies was someone I always looked up to. I was fortunate that when he came back to Rugby Union from Rugby League I had the privilege to play alongside him in the Welsh team. To look up to someone of his calibre and then to play alongside him, that was a special moment."

JD: "Your first cap must have been a special moment too"

DJ: "Yes, a fantastic moment actually. It was in '96 on the back of my first season with Bridgend. I'd had a very good season, as a young boy really. I was selected to go on the tour to Australia. Six and a half weeks away touring. I went there with no expectations. I was fortunate that someone dropped out in the first game. I played and managed to score. I was on the bench for the second test in Sydney, a nerve-wracking experience. Nigel Davies came off and I got my cap."

JD: "Which clubs have you played for?"

DJ: "I played for Bridgend first, then I went to Pontypridd and then down to Stradey. Then it was back to Bridgend which turned into the Celtic Warriors. The Warriors disbanded. I was left high and dry, so I went up to London to the Harlequins. Now I'm back with the Scarlets where I'm enjoying some of the best years of my life. It's a fantastic environment and a great place to play."

JD: "Are the people of Llanelli good supporters of the Scarlets?"

DJ: "Yes, very loyal supporters, especially when you're playing for them rather than against them. They've been quite hostile to some people, including me when I left the club. They turn up week in, week out in the rain and the shine. They're very passionate for their club."

JD: "What do you think of Welsh Rugby at the moment?"

DJ: "I think there's a lot to be done. Wales have done exceptionally well on occasions over the last few years, then let themselves down on other occasions. I think the structure of trying to develop the grass roots level has come on in leaps and bounds. I firmly believe the grass roots hold the key, but I think a little more marketing wouldn't go astray as well."

JD: "What do you think of the regional teams using overseas players?"

DJ: "I think for the likes of the Ospreys it's more of a marketing ploy. They've signed up the likes of Justin Marshall, high calibre, trying to draw more people in, which has worked. In fairness to him, he's playing well. It's the players who come here just for the ride that cripples the clubs. I think it's good if they can bring something along with them. Help to develop the younger players and give an insight into what's going on in countries like New Zealand, South Africa and Australia. I think it could be good for both parties then. As long as they're producing performances and helping younger players I'm all for it."

JD: "Do you think the number of overseas players should be restricted?"

DJ: "You've got to be careful with the numbers, but it could be restriction of fair trade as well. To limit the number of foreign players isn't a bad thing. If you look at the Zurich Premiership in England, where they've got an abundance of players, I don't think it's helping their national game. I'm sure something will be done about that before long. Have a few by all means, but try to develop your own players because that's the way forward."

JD: "Has anything disastrous or funny happened to you?"

DJ: "I've had highs and I've had lows. I was close to finishing when I had a problem with my shoulder. That was difficult to come to terms with on a mental level. That was a very low point in my career, but I fought it and luckily came through it. Funny things? There are a number of characters I've rubbed shoulders with. Garin Jenkins - I've got a lot of time for him. Dave Llewellyn is another. We were on a night out with Kingsley Jones, Mark Jones and a few others. At the end of the evening we were a bit peckish and went to a pizza parlour. Dave ordered a 12 inch Hawaiian and when it came the waiter asked Dave if he wanted it cut into four or eight pieces. Dave said, 'I'd better have four, I don't think I can eat eight'."

JD: "What are your future rugby plans?"

DJ: "Carry on with the Scarlets. I'm disappointed not to be in the Welsh setup at the moment, but I've still got aspirations. I was fortunate this year, I broke the European try scoring record. I'm delighted with that. There are things that I'm not in control of, like selection. All I can do is play my best and hope. I'm feeling fit, strong, powerful and sharp. I'd like to work on some aspects of my game. I think everybody can learn something, you're never too wise or too clever. I'm always trying to get an edge. I'm in a fortunate position, in a dream I suppose. Playing first class rugby and getting paid to do a job I love doing. I love training and it's a pleasure going to work. It's a fantastic lifestyle really. It's a daunting thought post-rugby, but it comes to us all I suppose. I think the key is to enjoy it. It's not as though I've squandered these years. I firmly believe I've got a fair few left too. Enjoy every moment, the highs and the lows,"

JD: "Is there a worst thing about being a professional?"

DJ: "The worst thing is when the media write negative things about you. I don't tend to read papers any more. They put you on a pedestal and then they want to knock you down. It can affect your family as well."

JD: "What does life hold for you after rugby?"

DJ: "There are a couple of things. I'd like to be my own boss, in the sporting field probably. I'm doing coaching courses and trying to finish a degree in Electronic Engineering with the Open University. I'm doing a bit of networking as well, with different companies, to see what doors will open."

JD: "What do you think about the move out of Stradey Park to a new stadium?"

DJ: "Stradey is synonymous with Welsh Rugby, but you have to move with the times. The stadium is a bit dilapidated now. You have to have a stadium which befits a top class team. The new stadium is not a million miles away. I think it will be a great facility. Stradey is a special place, but I'm sure this new stadium will be fantastic."

JD: "What would you like to have been if you hadn't played rugby?"

DJ: "I wouldn't have minded being a professional footballer or golfer. Something in the sports line anyway. I've thought of climbing a mountain as well or going on expeditions. Climbing Kilimanjaro or something like that would be quite nice."

JD: "Have you ever considered playing Rugby League?"

DJ: "I have actually. I did have a whisper that a couple of clubs were interested a few years ago. I thought it could have been a good experience. I didn't go for it, which was good really because things seemed to step up a gear for me in Rugby Union."

JD: "Anything you'd like to add?"

DJ: "Just a quote - Yesterday's history, tomorrow's a mystery and today's a gift. Seize the opportunity, seize the day."

It seems there are more saints than sinners in Wales. St. Tathan is the good lady whose name is commemorated in the village of St. Athan. Very little is known about her even though the biggest RAF base in Britain is also named in her honour.

We didn't see any planes, but pulling up at the junction ahead was a van with 'The Veg Rack' written on it. My mind immediately thought vegetarian until I noticed the words ' Greengrocery Deliveries'. You don't see many vans like that these days. The Tesco home delivery van regularly comes down our street. On the side of that is written, 'You shop, we drop'.

What's black when you buy it? Red when you use it? Grey when you throw it away? That should be easy if you're a miner's son like me. The answer is coal. overlooking the seashore, Aberthaw Power Station uses coal from Tower Colliery, Merthyr. It also burns biomass fuel and, in an effort to reduce pollution, has recently spent millions on a desulphurisation project.

Aberthaw also has a huge cement works as well as the Blue Anchor pub which sold its first pint of beer in 1380. We didn't stop to sample the beer, nor were we deterred by the low flying plane overhead as we flew past Cardiff airport.

We took a break on the outskirts of Barry. As we sat on a grassy bank in Tesco's car park the sun came out to play. On the other side of the road was Colcot School where I ran my first ever cross country race for Port Talbot Harriers in October 1983.

Why is envy green? The grass we sat on was green. Does that mean grass is green with envy? Tesco's toilet was very clean. It had a mirror with an envy-green circular surround. The other mirror had a raging-red frame around it.

Back on the bikes, I pointed out Jenner Park to Ian. Once a very successful Welsh League soccer team, Barry Town play there. It's also the home track of Barry and Vale Athletics club. When I first ran there, it had a black cinder surface. It was a warm, dry day and after the race we all looked like miners after a shift down the pit.

A long downhill lunge brought us to the heavily industrialized eastern edge of the town. The distillation columns of Dow Corning dominated the skyline like a mad Manhattan nightmare. Then, all of a sudden, we were in open countryside again. Dinas Powys came and went, then Penarth Marina arrived with the grand old Custom House behind and the brand new Cardiff Barrage in front.

I'd checked a map of the area which showed a road crossing the barrage and continuing into Cardiff East avoiding the city centre. The reality was that on the far side of the barrage was a large fence with a large, locked gate. On the gate was a sign which said, 'Cardiff Docks - Entry to authorised persons only'. "Oh! What do we do know?" said Ian. "We've got no choice", said I. "We'll have to go back and through the city centre."

From the barrage I'd hoped to use the coast roads through Cardiff and Newport, then the A48 from Caldicot to Chepstow. That was plan A. Time to implement plan B - get through Cardiff and find the A48 which I knew would take us directly to Chepstow.

I didn't have a street map of Cardiff, but I knew if we kept heading east we'd be ok. We cruised around Cardiff Bay, girdled the 'Golden Armadillo' that is the Millennium Centre, but the district of Splott splattered my sense of direction. Then I spotted a street sign which read 'Broadway'. I'd been to Broadway before. I bought my Fender Stratocaster in the music shop there. More importantly, I knew how to get to the A48 from Broadway.

Cardiff has been our capital city since December 20th, 1955. Thanks to the second Marquess of Bute, by 1913 Cardiff docks was the biggest exporter of coal in the world. Cardiff is also the birthplace of such diversely famous people as Roald Dahl, Ryan Giggs, Colin Jackson, Shirley Bassey, Ivor Novello and Charlotte Church.

We never went to church. Capel y Bedyddwyr, Bethania was our place of worship. It was only in the next street, but one cold, snow-covered Sunday my Dad said, "No chapel today, the road is too slippery." That night as he prepared to walk to the workingmen's club three streets away, I asked him was it not too slippery. His reply was, "I'll be careful".

We had to be careful on the A48 as well. For the first mile it was a dual carriageway and very busy. We cycled on the narrow hard shoulder which disappeared at the exit slip roads. I felt much happier when it became a quieter single carriageway.

***Transporter Bridge, Newport, Gwent***

On the outskirts of Newport, we took a break in the Tredegar Park Sports Ground. Sitting on a bench under a splendid conifer, we watched some kids kicking a football around. Behind us, the flat-roofed, orange-painted pavilion with its bright blue doors looked like a Caribbean beach house. From the crazy golf course came some excited screams and shouts as some crazy kids competed with the tricky traps.

Caerleon was the old port on the River Usk. As ships became bigger the port moved downstream and the 'Newport' became the centre for coal export and business. We skirted the city centre by sticking to the A48 which led us towards the docks area. This was a very busy road with loads of heavy vehicles. We made one stop so that I could photograph the Transporter Bridge. The bridge celebrates its centenary this year and is the biggest one of its type in the world. The high level frame allows ships to pass underneath while a gondola provides safe passage for pedestrians and vehicles. We crossed the Usk on the road bridge just up river.

Just beyond the docks we were saved by a cycle path alongside the road. This came to an end at the Coldra interchange where we dismounted and walked around to the A48. From here the cycling was more enjoyable. The road was wide, there was less traffic and there were quite a few long downhill stretches.

Soon, a sign said 'Chepstow 4 Miles'. Half a mile later another sign said 'Chepstow 4 Miles', we weren't discouraged. After a tough climb we freewheeled down a steep, twisting descent and turned left into Beaufort Square, Chepstow at 3.45pm.

***Chepstow Castle***

I'd made it, the end of the journey at last. Well, not quite, you're not getting off that easily. I'm going to detain you a little longer by telling you about our overnight stay and the journey home.

The data on the bike computer reckoned that we had cycled 70 miles, the longest trip on the journey. It had taken 5 hours and 35 minutes (not counting food breaks) at an average speed of 12.5mph. The maximum speed was an extraordinary 37.7mph. Where I achieved that on a loaded bike I'm not quite sure.

A short walk just a little further down the hill brought us to the First Hurdle guest house in Upper Church Street. We took our bikes straight through and chained them together in the walled back garden. There were two Siamese cats in the garden. I'd never seen cats like them before. They had chocolate brown stripes on their faces, legs and sides. One was quite friendly, the other just stuck his nose up in the air and walked off with a disdainful flick of his delicate tail.

After a shower and some refreshments, Ian said, "Dad, do you fancy cycling home tomorrow?"

I said, "Well, I had planned to, but if you don't want to it doesn't matter."

"It's a long way and the traffic was so bad around Cardiff and Newport," said Ian.

"You're right," I said. "I don't really fancy cycling home either. I've achieved my objective of getting to Chepstow. How we get home doesn't matter. We'll check out the trains later, but first let's take a look at the castle."

Yes, another castle. This is the last one now though. On the short walk to the castle, we passed an incongruously new building called Davis Court. Wrong spelling, so nothing to do with my family.

Chepstow Castle occupies a formidable defensive position on the cliff top overlooking the River Wye. Construction began in 1067, only a year after the Norman Conquest. An indication of its importance was that the builder, William Fitzosbern, used stone from the outset. Normally, they would build from wood first. Inevitably with such a large building, it was not completed until 1300.

Over the early years it was used as a base for subjugating the surrounding areas. During the Civil War it was held by the Royalists until their defeat by Cromwell who was granted ownership in 1648. After the Restoration in 1660, Henry Marten was imprisoned there for his part in the execution of Charles I. The tower where he was confined still retains the title of Marten's Tower. Chepstow Castle is now a well-maintained ruin and worth a visit.

We got to the castle at 5.40pm. It was closing at 6.00pm which didn't give us enough time to do it justice and I'd been there before anyway. We went into the gift shop where I bought a bookmark and a chocolate love spoon (a perfect combination!) for Ad.

Enough of castles. In the car park was an information board with details of the Offa's Dyke Footpath. I'd finally arrived at the southern end of it. If you cast your mind all the way back to chapter 2, I said as I passed through Prestatyn that turning left onto the trail there would have been a nice little short cut. It would have saved me about 300 miles, but then I wouldn't have seen all those other wonderful parts of Wales.

Our next port of call was the railway station where we discovered that a train for Cardiff would be leaving Chepstow at 9.27am the following morning. We could change there for Port Talbot or, if necessary, cycle the rest of the way home. We settled for that and headed back into the town.

In Beaufort Square there is a monolithic war memorial alongside which there is a naval gun. The gun is a memorial to ABS William C. Williams who is the only person from Chepstow to be awarded the Victoria Cross. Unfortunately he was killed in action at Gallipoli in 1915.

It was a pleasure to walk up the High Street, despite the steep slope. The paving has won a design award from the Worshipful Company of Paviours.

Incorporated at intervals between the paving slabs were coin bricks with replicas of old coins in them, plaques with details of old shops and their owners and bands of poetry. One of the bands had this inscription on it - 'Fins flash, beady-eyed bankers count coins on silver scales'. On one of a number of small roadside columns was written -

*A Chepstow salmon's worth his weight in gold*

*Unlike the flabby fish in London sold.*

We walked under the narrow town gate through which the main road once ran, then returned to the Hurdle.

It was too early to eat, so I went to have a look at St. Mary's Church at the end of the street while Ian phoned Tina, his girlfriend. It's a bit of a patchwork building, the new bits being clearly discernible from the older parts. As I stood admiring the Norman frontage, a man walked around the corner of the building towards me.

He stopped and pointing to the church said, "Bit of a hotch-potch, what?" He must have been in his 80s, but looked lean and upright with a bright spark in his eye. He was at least six feet tall and was dressed in what I'd call a country gent style. It might have been a shooting jacket that he wore.

I asked if he was interested in churches. His voice was strong and his manner supremely confident as he replied, "No, not at all. My interest is military campaigns, especially the Civil War. Henry Marten, a crony of Cromwell's, is buried here".

As the conversation continued, he revealed that he'd been an army officer and had fought in several campaigns himself. Sniffing a good story, I asked if he'd had any close shaves.

"One or two, but nothing I couldn't handle", he said. "I left the Army and, with no ties, found myself in Bolivia, must have been about 1950-51. The country wasn't very stable then and I got roped in to help the Nationalist Revolutionary Movement. The people were very poor and uneducated. The MNR, as it was known there, promised to help. I was in charge of a small force guarding a tin mine. I had to walk a short distance through the forest to get from my quarters to the mine. One day on this walk, a teenage boy jumped out in front of me with a pistol in his hand. I could see he was very nervous, his hand was shaking. My Spanish was quite good by this time and I understood that he wanted me to drop my gun belt and hand over my wallet. I did this, then said to him that I would look a fool to my friends if I told them that I'd been robbed by a boy. I took off my jacket, threw it on the floor and said, 'Please shoot into it so that I can say I had a lucky escape.' His eyes lit up and he fired three shots into my jacket. Then I took off my hat, threw that onto the floor and said, 'Please shoot my hat and then I can say a band of brigands robbed me.' He was really excited now and fired three more shots into my hat. Then I asked him, 'How many more bullets left in your gun?' Of course, he had none left, so I picked up my gun and pointing it at him said, 'Now please give me back my money'. He squealed, dropped the pistol and wallet and was away up the path like an express train."

Fortunately, I wasn't accosted by any Bolivian brigands on my way back to the First Hurdle. In reception, I spotted some books on a coffee table. I couldn't resist the temptation and was pleased to find a book called 'On Borrow's Trail' by Hugh Olliff and published by Gomer. (George Borrow published a book in 1862 called 'Wild Wales' telling of his travels around our beautiful country.)

Olliff wrote about Borrow's character as being egotistic and prejudiced.

During his stay in Chester, Borrow came upon an African former slave who earned his living preaching against slavery at religious meetings. Olliff states that Borrow's treatment of this person would be totally unacceptable today.

The point I'm coming to is that there is something of an eerie coincidence here. While I was in Chester, I also came across a person of African descent who was preaching and singing in the Town Hall Square. There, however, the similarity between me and Borrow ends. I practise tolerance.

We settled for the Jade Chinese restaurant in St Mary Street where there was a good vegetarian choice on the menu. Ian had spare ribs followed by Special Chow Mein. I had Mock Chicken (Tofu) with mixed vegetables and boiled rice. The Tiger Singapore lager also went down a treat. The background music was terrific too, a 60s compilation with bands like 'The Searchers' and 'Freddie and the Dreamers'. Poor old Freddie died recently at the age of 67. A very nice meal, with excellent service and pleasant surroundings.

The Beaufort Hotel had a giant screen for the England-Sweden World Cup soccer match, so we went straight there from the Chinese. After dominating the first half, England should have won comfortably. All credit to Sweden though, they came back and deserved the 2-2 draw. It was a game of two halves as they say.

I think we were the only Welsh people in the bar. The most common accent seemed to be that of the West Country. There was no trouble though. Everyone seemed to enjoy the game.

It was all downhill after that. A short walk downhill from the Beaufort to the Hurdle where we had an early night after a hard day's cycle.

# *Wednesday, 21ˢᵗ June*

*The sum of strategic determination*

*Is the practice of self flagellation*

*The failure to desist*

*Will certainly consist*

*Immediately in degradation*

$O$n this day in 1305 King Wenceslas II of Bohemia died; in 1854 the first ever Victoria Cross was awarded to Charles Davis Lucas; in 1905 Jean-Paul Sartre was born; in 1944 Ray Davies of the Kinks was born; in 1982 Prince William was born; this is also the longest day of the year being the summer solstice.

Don't tell me, the limerick above isn't the one you were expecting, right? It wasn't the one I was expecting either. I don't know where it came from, it just popped out of my mind complete, and if anyone can tell me what it means I'd be grateful. It was hard enough getting rhymes for Glamorgan and Port Talbot. Nothing rhymes with Margam, that's why I've used this last limerick.

Back in Chepstow, I'd run all the way to England and back by 7.30am. Luckily England was only the other side of the Wye. Ian had more sense, he stayed in bed. Breakfast was of the same high standard as I've come to expect on my travels. We finished our packing, then cycled over to the station. The main building was nicely constructed of dressed stone, but the corrugated steel roof was a bit of a mis-match I think. There was no ticket office either. I guessed that we'd have to pay on the train - I haven't been on a train in this country for years.

The Cardiff train was leaving from platform 1. Problem - we were on platform 2 and the only way across the line was via a footbridge. "Don't worry, Dad", said Ian, "I'll take my bike over first and come back to help with yours." My bike had four panniers and a bar bag on it while Ian's was unladen.

He scooted off and, always up for a challenge; I decided to give it a go on my own. I was half way up before Ian came back and determined to go it alone by then. It wasn't too difficult.

When the train arrived spot on time, it was a little two carriage affair without an engine to pull it. There was no guard's van (now I'm showing my age) either. I had to stand with my bike in the boarding space between two sets of double doors while Ian tucked his bike into the luggage space.

When the conductor came along, his eyes nearly popped out of his head. "There's not enough room here for a bike", was his incredulous reaction. I asked was there anywhere else to put it. He said there wasn't, but faced with a fait accompli because the train was well on its way by then, he said, "Oh all right, you can stay there then".

I asked for two singles to Port Talbot and also if we'd have to change at Cardiff. He said that the train was going through Bridgend and we could change there if we wanted to. Ian said he didn't mind cycling from Bridgend and I agreed. Later, the tannoy system announced that the train was actually going to Maesteg via Tondu. We activated Plan C then, because Tondu is even closer to home than Bridgend.

We passed through Newport and Cardiff a lot quicker than we had the day before. With only a short distance to go and nothing much happening, I thought I'd liven things up a bit by telling you about a writing competition that I entered a few years ago. The title was given and the story could not be more than 250 words. This is the story that I wrote :-

### *Flawed but Fatally Attractive*

*He had admired her from afar for some time now. Could he raise the courage to approach such a beautiful creature? Those long legs seemed to go on forever before reaching her voluptuous body.*

*Unsure at first, but driven by a powerful inner compulsion, he made his move. Her raven-black hair glistened in the sunlight as he drew near. Suddenly, their eyes met and there was a mutual understanding. Could this be true, was he about to enter the emotional Eden of his dreams?*

*They caressed silently, enjoying the closeness of their intimate embrace. He possessed her completely now and a quiver ran through his frame with the climax of his passion.*

*As he relaxed, he felt a sudden change in her attitude. He tried to leave the web, but her eight long legs gripped him tightly as she slowly injected the poison into his struggling body.*

**The wanderers return**

I hope you liked it. At Tondu, we got off the train and it took us 43 minutes to cycle the eight miles home to Margam. My great bike journey was over at 11.45am on 21st June, 2006, the longest day of the year, but the shortest trip of the tour.

For those who like details, I've scientifically measured, with the aid of a map, a piece of string and a ruler, most of the distances of each stage. The last two stages were measured using the bike computer :-

| | |
|---|---|
| Chester to Llandudno | 51 miles |
| Llandudno to Cemaes Bay | 53 miles |
| Cemaes Bay to Caernarfon | 50 miles |
| Carnarfon to Criccieth | 57 miles |
| Criccieth to Aberdyfi | 45 miles |
| Aberdyfi to Aberaeron | 46 miles |
| Aberaeron to Croesgoch | 52 miles |
| Croesgoch to Tenby | 41 miles |
| Tenby to Carmarthen | 37 miles |
| Carmarthen to Port Talbot | 56 miles |
| Port Talbot to Chepstow | 70 miles |
| Tondu to Margam | 8 miles |
| TOTAL | 566 miles |

Before I finish I'd like to pass on some sage advice that my Gran gave me when I was very young and I've always been careful to stick to it since. She said, "Now remember, boy, don't you ever go taking a laxative and a sleeping potion on the same night".

The Great Philosopher once said that life is like a tin of pilchards. I'm off to find the key now.

## END

# Photograph Index

Lightning Source UK Ltd.
Milton Keynes UK
UKOW02f2358210316

270600UK00001B/34/P